Son of stitch 'n bitch

SON of Stitch'N'bitch

45 Projects to Knit & Crochet for **MEN**

debbie stoller

Fashion Photography by Anna Wolf • Illustrations by Adrienne Yan

WORKMAN PUBLISHING • NEW YORK

For Michael,
who's been there for me through all the stitching,
and all the bitching.

Copyright © 2007 by Debbie Stoller
Photography copyright © 2007 Anna Wolf
Additonal photography by Tod Seelie and Jenna Bascom
Illustrations copyright © 2007 Adrienne Yan

Library of Congress Cataloging-in-Publication Data

Stoller, Debbie.
    Son of stitch 'n bitch: 45 projects to knit & crochet for men / by Debbie Stoller.
        p. cm.
    Includes index.
    ISBN-13: 978-0-7611-4617-9 (alk. paper)
1.   Knitting—Patterns. 2. Men's clothing. I. Title.
    TT825.S748 2007
    746.43'2041—dc22   2007038085

Workman books are available at special discounts when purchased in bulk for premiums and sales promotions as well as for fund-raising or educational use. Special editions or book excerpts can also be created to specification. For details, contact the Special Sales Director at the address below.

Design by Janet Vicario with Munira Al-Khalili

WORKMAN PUBLISHING COMPANY, INC.
225 Varick Street
New York, NY 10014-4381
www.workman.com

Printed in the United States of America
First printing October 2007

10 9 8 7 6 5 4 3 2 1

Acknowledgments

So many people helped to make this book come into being, and I want to thank them in the order in which they became involved.

First, I wish to thank my talented editor, Ruth Sullivan, for being behind this project from the get-go, and express my gratitude to Peter Workman, for agreeing that the book should be written. Once again, I am so very indebted to my wonderful agent, Flip Brophy, for getting the deal done.

I owe an immense thanks to my own personal Jill of All Trades, Jennifer Wertkin, who helped me organize the overwhelming number of submissions received, did an amazing job of coordinating between the designers and the yarn companies, made herself available for last-minute deadline knitting sessions, and just basically served as my right-hand gal in all things Stitch 'n Bitch. I am truly grateful. I am also thankful to the Y-chromosome peer review committee of Vinnie D'Angelo (who also served as impromptu mannequin for in-progress and completed projects), Peter Stoller, and Michael Uman, for helping with the project selection process.

As always, the designers who came up with such clever and beautiful ideas for this book deserve the largest thanks. They were all willing to work and at times rework their projects until they were completely perfect, and this book owes so much to their tireless and creative efforts. I am extremely grateful for the opportunity to feature their work in this book.

Most of the projects in this book were knit by the designers themselves, but for some it was necessary to call in helping hands, so I wish to thank my knitting and crocheting brigade: Marney Anderson, Eileene Coscolluela, Sue DiMora, Ellen Hauser, Whitney Hess, Buffi Jashanmal, and Jennifer Wertkin.

I always enjoy being a part of the photo shoots for my books; it's when I finally get to see everything come together, with the help of a large and talented group of people. For this book, it was Art Director Janet Vicario who did an immense amount of work overseeing the entire shoot, and I am deeply grateful for her creative eye and wonderful understanding of how these projects should best be shown. Photographer Anna Wolf made the boys look cute and natural in their knit and crochet wear, stylist JenniLee did an amazing job of getting the look just right, hair stylist and makeup artist Rita Madison got everyone looking perfect, and Photo Director Leora Kahn and her assistants, Jenna Bascom and Sofia Tome, helped to wrangle the adorable models. Speaking of whom, this book wouldn't be nearly as fun to look at if it weren't for the handsome, hunky hotties who adorn its pages, so a special thanks to the models who appear here: Dar, Khi, Tet, Todd, and Luis.

I just love working with Eve Ng, and I'm so glad she was available to be the Technical Editor on this book. She did such a wonderful and thorough job of going through the "knitty"-gritty of each pattern. And I truly appreciate Edie Eckman's work as an eagle-eyed second Technical Editor. I want to thank Adrienne Yan for the cute illustrations that support the text. Copy editor Judit Bodnar is not just a wordsmith but also a knitter and I'm so grateful for her careful attention to detail, and tireless Production Editor Irene Demchyshyn coordinated the entire project and made sure the book got out on time. I'm also grateful to design assistant Munira Al-Khalili for working on the many charts and schematics that appear in the book and to the typesetting/pre-press whiz Jarrod Dyer for his technical and visual assistance. They were mentioned before, but the two people who worked the hardest on getting the words and the layouts together for the book you see here are my incredible editor Ruth Sullivan and the wonderfully talented Janet Vicario—I can't thank them enough for their hard work on this project.

I've dedicated this book to my long-time partner, Michael Uman. He's been my biggest cheerleader for many years, and I am more grateful for his solid support and generous love than any pair of hand-knit socks could ever express.

Contents

The Patterns (CONTINUED)

PART I
i know what boys like
Knitting for Men

Question any group of stitchers on their experiences knitting or crocheting for men and you're likely to hear a variety of horror stories—about projects that took months to make but were never worn, about the sense of futility and rejection felt by the knitter in question, about how men just don't appreciate handmade items, or about the man who refused to wear a hat that was made with "heathered" yarn because Heather is a girl's name. You might also hear tell of the dreaded "sweater curse," the one that holds that if you knit your boyfriend a sweater, it pretty much guarantees the end of the relationship.

Whether it's made for a (possibly soon-to-be-ex) boyfriend, or a husband, father, son, or nephew, projects made for men appear to be rejected at a higher rate than those made for women. And yet, for much of knitting's history, the majority of knit goods, whether produced by men's or women's hands, were made for—and definitely worn by—men. Caps, mittens, socks, and sweaters—all have their origins as menswear, and sweaters in particular are a relatively recent addition to women's wardrobes, while they have been a mainstay of men's for centuries (see page 8).

So what gives? Why are today's men so difficult to knit for? Why won't they wear what we knit for them? And most important, how can we get them to start wearing the things we make? The answer is simple: If you want a man to wear what you've made, make him something that he likes. Because no matter how much he likes (even loves) you, that feeling will not transfer to a project that you slaved over if he thinks that it is too big, too small, too itchy, not his color, not his style, too feminine, too conservative, too nerdy, too wild, too youthful, too baggy, not baggy enough, or whatever else he—*just like you*—considers before choosing an item of clothing for his wardrobe.

Yet, this obvious answer can be quite challenging in practice. For one thing, many women don't realize that the men in their lives, no matter how slovenly, actually think of themselves as *having* a style. But the fact is that even that guy who is never seen in anything other than a T-shirt, jeans, and zip-up jacket has a definite sense of things that he will and won't wear. He has certain colors that he likes and others that he dislikes. He is particular about how loose or snug he likes to wear his T-shirts, and whether his hoodies should come to his hips or stop at his waist. He knows

A NOTE TO THOSE READERS WHO ARE MAN ENOUGH TO KNIT:

Few developments in the knitting community have been more exciting and gratifying to me than seeing so many men take up the needles lately— I love that knitting is finally beginning to shake the stigma of being too girly for guys. But if you're one of the few, the proud, the men with balls (of yarn), you should probably step along—there's not much for you to see here. This intro was written to help the womenfolk understand how to knit for you, since that is a task that can be fraught with so many pitfalls for them. But seeing as you are a bona fide male of the species, you of course already know what you like in a project, you know what colors you like, and you know what size you like to wear. You might want to check out the section titled "Precautionary Measures" (page 14) to find out how to alter a pattern so that it matches one of your favorite sweaters in fit, but otherwise, please proceed directly to the pattern section. I'll see you there!

whether he wants to emphasize his well-developed chest or hide his lack of one, and makes sure that none of his clothes call attention to his beer belly or to the fact that he is no taller than Tom Cruise.

Of course, male knitters know all this already. They also know something else that confronts knitters of both genders who are looking to make men's projects: There just aren't that many patterns to choose from, and, of the patterns that are available, many are overwrought with bobbles and cables or too many color panels or are just plain *wrong* in some way. That's

often because these projects have been designed from the perspective of the knitter or crocheter rather than that of the wearer: They may be satisfying and fun to make because of their intricate cabling or challenging color work, but, unfortunately, they are not necessarily what most men are willing to wear.

In fact, if you look for a moment at the men around you—at work, in the mall, on the street—you'll see that, for the most part, men like to dress simply. They like navy blue, gray, khaki, olive, and black; and sweaters, if they wear them, are done up in plain stitches such as stockinette or ribbing. In fact, as I write this at a café in Brooklyn, the men around me are exclusively dressed in these colors and styles: Two are sporting navy blue hoodies, two are wearing zip-up, ribbed, charcoal gray cardigans, one is wearing a black V-neck sweater, and another is wearing a ribbed black turtleneck. Yet, how boring would it be to knit such a sweater, especially given the fact that men's sweaters usually take so much

Grounds for Divorce? I made a beautiful Aran pullover as a surprise for my first husband's birthday just after we were married. It sat in his drawer and I could never get him to let me see how it looked on him. We separated a year later and one day at my lawyer's I was given a note from my ex saying that, among other things, he hated the fact that I made him a sweater and never even bothered to measure him for it. Turns out the neck was too tight and he couldn't pull it over his head. I hate to think that's why he wanted a divorce, but you never know. By the way, he gave me back the sweater as part of the divorce settlement, so I frogged it and made a dog sweater for our poodle. Sandi S, Colme, SD

time to make? Spending evening after evening, weekend upon weekend, relegated to knitting nothin' but stockinette in gray wool might seem like punishment to most experienced knitters, the equivalent of sitting in a dark room with the windows closed and the shades drawn on a gorgeous spring day.

With so much beautiful yarn to work with, and so many fun stitches to make, why limit yourself to making miles and miles of knit 2, purl 2 in drab olive worsted? Well, I'll tell you why: Because that's what *he* wants. Because that's what he likes to wear. He's not a dog you can dress in whatever you think will make him look cute; he's not a child who isn't able to make decisions for himself; and he certainly isn't a lump of clay, waiting to be transformed, by your deft stitcher's hands, into a sturdy, strong-but-sensitive type who will sport a heavily cabled off-white fisherman sweater, or a hipster who will ironically wear a turquoise-and-green argyle mohair vest, even if it does flatter his skin tone and make his eyes seem to sparkle. My point is, choosing a project to stitch for a guy is no time to make like Henry Higgins and try to My-Fair-Lady his ass. A man (like a woman) likes what he likes. Your job is simply to find out what that is.

That's where this book comes in. Each of the projects here was either designed by a man or designed in collaboration with a man. Nonknitting men were consulted throughout the design selection process to determine which projects most appealed to them (and, more important, which ones they'd actually wear), and contributors were directed to check their design ideas

with the men in their lives. Only projects that were given the thumbs-up by a variety of men made the cut; and as you will see, that includes a great assortment of styles. Yet not only are these patterns 100 percent boy-approved, but they are also fun enough to maintain a knitter or crocheter's interest for the long haul—which, if you're working on an oversized sweater for a dude, can be quite a long haul indeed. Some of the projects are rather conservative in design; others are high-concept pieces or incorporate a sense of humor; and still others are somewhat sporty—and each can be worn by a great number of different kinds of menfolk.

Tea for Two I believed in the curse, and knew I couldn't risk making my boyfriend a sweater, so I went instead for a hat. It was beautiful, knit in a pricey yarn, soft and stripey and funky and warm. I even went wool wild, and made a pom-pom the size of an orange for the top of the hat. I wrapped it and mailed it off to him, and he called to thank me, somewhat generically. The next time I went to his house, he offered to make tea while I sat down and relaxed. When he arrived with the laden tray, there, in the center, misshapen and drenched with hot steam, was my stylish hat—serving as a freaking teapot cozy! **Anonymous**

As you review these patterns with the men in your life in mind, try to *look beyond* the pictured project and think how you might tailor it to suit your recipient. First and foremost, look at the style and fit (meaning, the overall shape of the piece), and think of the given color choices as mere suggestions. An orange, brown, and tan hoodie could just as easily be done in all-over gray or red, white, and blue; a grass green hat could be worked up in navy blue. Try to look past the models, too: The sweater worn here by a cute hipster dude, who looks like he'd be most comfortable on a motorcycle, might be just the thing for your dad, who'd be most comfortable on a golf course (or, for that matter, in a La-Z-Boy). And unless the project is intended to be a surprise, get your man involved in the process. Ask him which project appeals to him, what color he'd like it to be, and measure his favorite sweater to guarantee a great fit (more on this later). And if you do want to keep what you're making a surprise, launch a covert fact-finding mission to gather this information—or the surprise just might be on you.

i knit it my way
A Cautionary Tale

The first project I ever made for a man was shortly after I'd become obsessed with knitting and crocheting. Using some leftover chunky maroon yarn, with a nice sheen and just a touch of mohair, I hooked up a plain, double-crochet-stitch scarf for my boo. While the scarf would be easy for me to make today, at the time it took all of my concentration to keep from increasing or decreasing my stitches on every row, and I presented it to him with a great sense of pride. Certain that he'd be excited to receive something that I'd made with my very own hands, and secure in the knowledge that the color was a becoming choice for his deep olive skin, it was with quite a

bit of disappointment that I realized, after a number of weeks, that the thing had never been worn. "Oh, I'd never wear purple," the man said matter-of-factly when asked why he had chosen to ignore the little bit o' love I'd whipped up for him. "It's not purple, it's maroon!" I countered. "Whatever," he replied, "I'd never wear that color." Until he'd said it, it had never occurred to me that this man *had* colors—most of his wardrobe consisted of items that were black, gray, or blue, and I'd assumed that was the result of his being too lazy to take a wilder ride around the color wheel when choosing his clothing.

So on my next attempt, I decided to be more careful. I found a pattern for a simple, loose-fitting pullover with an interesting knit-and-purl pattern. It was a modern gansey, the kind of thing I thought my man would like, and I got his approval on the design before I started. Burned by my previous negative experience, this time around I knew enough to make the thing in gray, and followed the directions for the extra-large size, since that's the size of his clothing. I worked on

Deal-Breaker I knit the Skully sweater for my boyfriend at the time. We broke up in late May. (I do not blame the Sweater Curse at all. Seriously, I don't.) Apparently for the next two weeks he wore the sweater almost constantly, despite the warm weather, and when girls commented on how great it was, he told them that *he had knitted it himself.* I told him that if any boy told me he'd knitted a sweater and then I found out it was actually his ex-girlfriend who made it, that would be a total deal-breaker. Monstrosity, Ontario, CAN

My Heart Belongs to Daddy Last year, when I was a madly in love 16-year-old, I began knitting my very first real scarf for my boyfriend. They should change the sweater curse to the sweater/ scarf curse because days after I completed it, we broke up. I gave it to him anyway, complete with a little duplicate-stitched heart, but since he's away at college, I don't see him anymore, so there's no way to tell whether or not he wears it. From now on, the only man I'll knit for is my daddy because no curse could take him away from me. Jessica Siciliano, Hickory, NC

it diligently for months, again imagining how happy I'd be to see him wearing something I'd made. But alas, as soon as he tried on the completed garment, it was clear that something had gone terribly wrong. The thing stretched tight across his belly, the absolutely last part of his body he wanted to emphasize, and it wasn't long enough either, landing awkwardly at his waist. Desperate to salvage at least some of the work I'd done, I knit four extra pieces, in exactly the same knit-and-purl stitch pattern as the sweater, and sewed them to each side of the front and back to make the sweater wider. To make the sweater longer, I unraveled the bottom edge, then spent many a frustrating weekend trying to get the knit-and-purl pattern I was knitting downward to match the one above it.

It was a long time before I learned that, when knitting downward, your stitches are offset by half a stitch from the stitches in the rows above them, and you'll *never* be able to match them to the stitches above. So, instead, I cast on stitches and knit up, then attached this new "bottom" to the old bottom edge of the sweater. Finally, it was done. And it fit—it was both wide enough and long enough for my man. He even wore it a few times, but it was obvious he was only doing it to spare my feelings, and after a short time it took up residence at the bottom of his closet, never to be worn again. Truth be told, I couldn't really blame him. With seams running every which way but loose, and stitch patterns that only kinda-sorta matched up on the many pieces that I'd sewn together, it looked more like a quilt than a sweater. Not a good look for a guy—or for anyone, really.

But this story does have a happy ending. The next time I attempted a project for the boy, I tried something on a smaller scale: I chose gray again, this time springing for a gorgeous, tweedy cashmere-blend yarn. I worked up a simple mistake-rib scarf and a pair of matching fingerless gloves. This practical project, rugged-looking but with a secret hint of luxury, and made in his favorite clothing color, was a hit. He still wears them to this day, more than making up for the many lost hours I'd spent on his Frankensweater and allowing me to finally experience the pride and pleasure of seeing my man in something I'd knit especially for him. Not only that, but I'd also learned some valuable lessons about knitting for men.

Or so you'd think. When it came time to knit something for my father, I found a nice, affordable, tweedy forest-green yarn with flecks of black that looked a bit like the flannel shirts he liked to wear, and located a pattern for a zip-up bomber-jacket–style sweater that seemed dad-ish. And although this man

men in knits The First 800 Years

These days it can be a challenge to find something to knit that a man will wear, but for most of knitting's history, that was not a problem. Hand-knit caps, stockings, gloves, and sweaters were all worn by men long before they were ever put onto the bodies of women. It was only after machine knitting was well-established, and knitting became a leisure-time activity for the upper classes, that women had the opportunity to knit mostly fashionable items for themselves, with an occasional item made for their men. But even during this time, working-class women were still knitting their hands off to clothe their men or to bring in a bit of household money. And not only were most items knit for men, but much early knitting was done by men themselves.

Some of the oldest items that were made by the technique we now know as knitting date back to A.D. 1200. These were socks, knit in the round, although for whose feet they were intended is anybody's guess. But by the early 1400s, the first caps were being knit, and we know they were definitely intended for men, as they were designed to be worn under steel military helmets. Resembling contemporary men's earflap caps, they were most likely made by other men, as knitting in those days was done in organized guilds by men who were considered artisans (the first "Stitch 'n Britches"). These guilds also produced wonderfully ornate purses and gloves that were, you guessed it, carried and worn by other men. The gloves were known as "liturgical gloves"

and were mostly worn by the clergy. As long as oven mitts, they came complete with their own bling—ornamental rings knit right onto the fingers.

By the 1500s, men were all about knit silk stockings—thigh high, no less—and they continued to wear these until trousers came into fashion sometime after the French Revolution. Imelda Marcos's footwear fetish had little on King Erik of Sweden, who is said to have possessed twenty-seven pairs of hand-knit stockings. Knee socks were being knit as well, but they were reportedly worn only by children and artisans. "I think my leg would show well in silk hose," a male character says in a play of the time, and I'm certain the women of the time would have agreed. In fact, by the 1600s, silk stockings had become all the rage among upper-class men, and at least fifty shades of stockings were being produced in France for their lovely legs—including such colors as "dying monkey," "merry widow," "resuscitated corpse," and "kiss me darling." Apparently, however, there were no "nude" stockings to be had.

During the same period, men's undergarments were also hand knit, including a bizarre item called "trunk hose"—tight, short pants the length of swim trunks, with numerous vertical slits knit into them, perhaps for greater ease of movement, or perhaps for ventilation. Either way, they were pretty dang sexy. Knit undershirts, the precursors of sweaters, were also worn, and a gorgeous sky

A 16th-century gentleman sports over-the-knee hose. Below: Gloves made of knitted silk and silver-gilt thread, 16th-century Spain.

blue one in a fine knit-and-purl pattern was donned by King Charles for his execution in 1649.

Shortly thereafter, fishermen living on the Shetland Isles began wearing their underwear as outerwear (take that, Madonna!), and it was a good idea, too, since these early sweaters gave them the ease of movement that their work required. Until they figured this out, they'd been wearing woven shirts that were made larger than necessary, then carefully gathered around the top with an embroidery stitch that allowed it to stretch. This garment was known as a "smock" and the stitch is still known as smocking, although today it is used almost exclusively on tube-top dresses. Dutch whalers, who traded with the Shetlanders, continued to wear smocks, but eventually realized the islanders were onto something. Although it took them a couple hundred years to catch on, by the early 1800s they, too, were wearing sweaters.

By the mid-1800s, fishermen's sweaters were well established among the Dutch, and they had developed their own style and traditions. Mostly knit in a readily available dark blue yarn (which may be the origin of "navy blue"), they were worked in simple knit-and-purl patterns, and every seafaring town had its own motifs. More than just a matter of local pride, the specific motif could help identify the seaman's homeport or family if he were to be lost at sea. This tradition was carried on for many years. Even as late as 1939, it was reported that a Dutch sailor had drowned and had washed ashore, and

although his body was totally unidentifiable, his wife recognized her work in her husband's sweater. Another story tells of a number of sailors lost at sea whose sweaters were recovered and returned to their wives, who buried the garments.

Dutch fishermen from the towns of Scheveningen and Urk in their sweaters, circa 1910.

In nineteenth-century Ireland, knitted motifs in sailors' sweaters carried other messages as well, such as the number of sons in the man's family or his religious beliefs. In fact, the "God's Eye," a sort of cross motif that was very popular at the time, was put there as much to bring good luck to the men who wore them, as it was to remind them to behave themselves when they were off in foreign ports. Naughty boys!

Not all men's sweaters were utilitarian, though. In some Dutch towns, men had two sweaters: a thick one for work, which was often felted, and a thinner one for Sunday wear. The Sunday sweater was frequently a wedding gift from his bride. In fact, in Holland it was traditional for a bride to begin knitting this sweater for her betrothed on the day the wedding date was set. Similarly, in Britain, the future bride of a fisherman began knitting this special sweater as soon as she was engaged—and not a moment before. Could this be the origin of the sweater curse?

While women were wearing knit stockings, gloves, and shawls, as well as other knit goods, by the mid-nineteenth century, sweaters remained pretty much exclusively menswear. The popularity of certain styles can even be traced to specific menfolk: Cardigans were named for the Earl of Cardigan, and raglan sleeves were named for Lord Raglan. For a brief period, however, fisherman's sweaters became a fashion statement beyond the dockside, and in the 1880s women were wearing something called a "fisherman jersey," which had puffy sleeves, a tight waist, and a high neckline to resemble a woman's blouse. While it was certainly more comfortable than a blouse for those daring women who

Edward VIII sports the Fair Isle sweater that launched a fashion craze.

were taking up the modern sport of bicycling, it was not a good look and the fad quickly passed.

Things changed, however, in the Edwardian era. The dawn of the "physical culture" movement, which encouraged folks to get out of their dark Victorian drawing rooms and exercise, led to a new desire for wearable, movable clothing. Sweaters were no longer working-class wear and became *the* look for men who were out "motoring" or engaging in the newfangled game of golf. In fact, golfing plays an important role in the history of knitwear, believe it or not: It was on a golf course in 1922 that Edward VIII, the Prince of Wales, wore a beautiful Fair Isle sweater and started a craze for the style. And by the 1920s, women who had fought for—and won—the right to vote, also fought for—and won—the right to dress as comfortably as men. As they chopped off their long locks, undid their corsets, and slipped into simple, straight dresses, they also began pulling on brightly patterned sweaters, which suited the new masculine silhouette that was so in vogue. Not only were they fashionable, but sweaters were also by far the most comfortable thing for women to wear as they took to the golf courses and tennis courts beside their men. These sweaters often adopted the V-neck style, which itself originated in menswear design to show off a necktie.

By the 1930s, men and women were wearing knitwear to an equal degree. And while machine-knit clothing was easy to obtain, women continued to pick up their needles—for some it was a way to earn a bit more income for their working-class families or to save money on store-bought goods, for others it was a great way to relax or spend their newfound leisure time. And women of all classes took to the needles during times of war—specifically, to knit socks for men on the front lines. This tradition dates way back; American women knit for their soldiers who fought in the War of 1812, and for the Union and Confederate soldiers during the Civil War. In the 1850s, British women knit socks and mittens for men fighting the Crimean War, and they knit socks, scarves, knee warmers, and balaclavas for soldiers on the front lines of the Boer War, despite the fact that these men were fighting in the hot climate of South Africa. And during World Wars I and II, socks were knit so tirelessly by so many pairs of hands (both male and female) on every side of the conflict that it brought a resurgence in the popularity of knitting for many years after.

Inherent in wartime sock knitting is the sentiment that goes into knitting for a man—the belief that a hand-knit item

AMERICAN RED CROSS

OUR BOYS NEED
SOX
KNIT YOUR BIT

can somehow bring more comfort than one that is machine-made. Of course, this sense of loving purpose also gives pleasure to the knitter. It is a sentiment that was well understood by the many American women who became caught up in a late-nineteenth-century knitting craze of making silk cravats for their men. "All girls, young and old, fiancées, sweethearts, wives and mothers, love to make something *themselves* that the men whom they adore will wear!" a women's magazine writer of the time noted. "To see the man that one is interested in, or that one loves, wearing something worked for *him alone,* appeals to the best side of one's nature." It's an old idea that, over a century later, knitters can still relate to.

From left to right: Wounded World War I soldiers knit for the men on the front lines; Columbia undergrads take up the needles during a 1930s knitting craze; World War II soldiers, themselves wearing hand-knit vests, knit to pass the time.

would never be accused of having anything even approximating a "fashion sense," I knew that he had specific requirements, most notably the need for a breast pocket to accommodate the huge number of pens and pencils, along with assorted eyeglass cases, that he carried with him at all times, and so I added one to the pattern. Since I'd so carefully taken his tastes and needs into consideration, the sweater was a success—so much so that he wore it to death, which was more than the acrylic/wool blend yarn I'd bought (on sale) could really stand up to. It pilled like a mofo and looked ragged in no time.

So I decided it was time to upgrade. I found some real merino wool in navy blue, and, since my knitting skills had advanced by then as well, chose a more complicated cable-pattern. Again, I made sure it had pockets in the right place, and, after many, many months, finally managed to complete the beast. My father was once again a gracious recipient, only this time it was obvious that the sweater was much too big on him. The sleeves passed his knuckles, and it bagged so badly that his pencils could barely stay in their pockets, clattering to the ground whenever he bent over. If only I had made sure that the fit of the cabled cardigan matched that of the much-loved bomber jacket, I could have chalked up another knitting victory. But, instead, my father always leaves that sweater hanging in his closet, preferring, much to my mother's chagrin, to wear the very pilly acrylic one.

With sock knitting, however, you'd think one couldn't go wrong with my dad, as he is one of the few men in the twenty-first century who still wears hand-knit socks almost every day. That's because, when she was alive, my grandmother used to knit him a few pairs of socks a year, and to this day he continues to wear the ones she made him, even though some of them are over a decade old (my mother even darns them for him).

The first time I knit him a pair of plain gray socks, and saw how much he loved to wear them, I figured my days of searching for the perfect gift for the "man who hates everything" were finally a thing of the past. With hand-knit socks for his birthday, Father's Day, and Hannukah, I was guaranteed gift-giving glory. But that's when I jumped the shark. If gray socks were good, I thought, then patterned socks were better: I knit up a pair in self-patterning sock yarn in the manly colors of navy, tan, and gray. Of course, they were no more difficult to make than the first pair. But as far as my father was concerned, they were fancy socks, to be worn only on special occasions. He wore the fancy socks to my

The Socks Addict Knitting for a guy? I made that mistake once, and it now consumes most of my knitting time! My boyfriend so loves the socks that I knit him, that as soon as he starts wearing through a pair, he looks at whatever I am making for myself, makes a sweet and pitiful face, and says, "If you get bored or frustrated with that, I'd love a new pair of socks." I got so frustrated with him once that I knit him the most hideous pair of purple, green, and pink acrylic socks in hopes that he would get turned off from hand-knit socks and stop bugging me for a few months. He still loved them! Alicia Astin, Spins 'n Needles, Ottawa, CAN

grandmother's funeral (he thought that she, being the consummate sock knitter, would appreciate that), and sometimes he puts them on for Passover, but mostly, they are just passed over—left at the back of his sock drawer. The moral of the story? Not only should you pay attention to color, fit, and fiber when stitching for men, but even a little embellishment can make a project unwearable in the eyes (or to the feet) of many a man.

ſize Matterſ
Getting the Right Fit

As my man-knitting fiascos prove, the number-one thing to consider when making a project for a man is fit. After all, isn't that the most important thing you look for in your own clothing? The good news is that if you are making a hat, scarf, or mittens, you don't need to worry about fit very much. Obviously, a scarf can be wound around any size neck, and mittens or gloves can stretch to fit a variety of man-hands. As for hats, the average circumference of an adult male's head is 22", and since knitting is quite forgiving, knit hats can contract or expand to comfortably fit a somewhat smaller or larger head. Crochet is usually less stretchy, so if you are working a crocheted project, you might want to check your man's head measurement against the hat's size, and add or subtract a few stitches for a better fit.

When it comes to a sweater, though, size *definitely* matters. And in the world of men's clothing, size is a state of mind. Small, Medium, and Large are pretty much meaningless, because the size a man likes to

🧶 The Gift That Keeps on Giving
Many years ago I knit a green and orange afghan for my brother. Now he is close to retirement, and often wakes at 2 A.M., unable to get back to sleep. He gets out of bed, sits in a chair, and wraps himself in the warm, soft afghan. He says it relaxes him, and he is able to go back to bed and fall asleep. I am glad to know that something I knit many years ago still brings comfort to someone dear to me.
June Kinerson, Averil Park, NY

wear is often more a matter of personal preference than of actual measurements. Some men like their clothes loose and comfy—that's their style. So, for example, a man with a medium-size chest might constantly buy himself sweaters that are size Large. Thus, taking your man's actual measurements will only get you so far. You need to measure a favorite sweater as well to really get an understanding of how large or small to make your project. In fact, if you had to choose only one of these, the measurements from a favorite sweater will give you the best indication of what size sweater your guy will actually wear.

The difference between a person's actual measurements and the measurements of an item of clothing is called *ease.* So if a man has a chest that's 40" around, but his sweater measures 23" from armpit to armpit (46" in circumference) that means he likes his clothes to have about 6" of ease. This makes for a nice, loose-fitting sweater, one that may make a small-chested man look a bit bigger and hide any evidence of a beer belly. On the other hand, he might prefer a more conservative fit—perhaps only about 2" of ease—so he'd wear a 42" sweater, which would lie closer to his body and show off all those hours he's been spending at the gym after work.

Of course, how an item of clothing is meant to be worn also affects the amount of ease it requires: A sweater that is intended to be pulled on over a T-shirt doesn't need as much ease as does a cardigan or hoodie that is going be worn over a button-up shirt or possibly even a sweatshirt. Finally, the thickness of the yarn you are going to use influences the amount of ease as well: A sweater made in chunky yarn will require more ease than one made in a thinner yarn, because the thickness of the yarn actually eats up some of that air space between a man's body and his clothing. That's why measuring a favorite sweater will give you the best idea of what size to make your project—it already incorporates the man's preferred amount of ease.

precautionary measures
Getting Numbers from a Man's Sweater

Start with a sweater that is similar to the project you are planning to make—a pullover or cardigan, for instance. By the way, if you're not close enough to a man to be able to measure one of his sweaters, or ask someone who lives with him to do it, then you're not close enough to knit him a sweater. Try a one-size-fits-all project like a hat or scarf instead. Trust me on this one.

For sweater width, lay the sweater flat, and measure it across the chest at the widest point, just below where the sleeves start. Double that number; this gives you the circumference of the sweater (not the man's chest). Make the pattern size that has a finished chest measurement closest to this size. You might be tempted to adjust the pattern to measure this size *exactly,* but if you're dealing with any kind of color work or cable pattern, it'll take too much futzing to get everything to work out at your new stitch count. If you're up for that kind of torture, good on ya; otherwise, just select the closest finished measurement and you should be fine.

The other measurements to be concerned with are sweater length and sleeve length—and both are relatively easy to adjust.

For sweater length, measure from the top of the shoulder to the bottom of the sweater. Look at the schematic for the sweater you are planning to make and see how well your measurement, well,

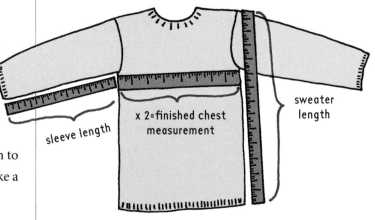

sleeve length

x 2=finished chest measurement

sweater length

measures up. If yours is shorter, or longer, determine by how much (for instance, your sweater is 3" shorter than the one in the book or 2" longer). You'll make this adjustment on the sweater as you work your way up to the armpit, where the pattern will usually instruct you to bind off stitches on either side of the front and back. If you're working a sweater with drop sleeves, meaning the sweater front or back has no "bite" in the sides for a sleeve to fit into, you can make that adjustment anywhere along the side of the sweater, as long as it's before the neck shaping. Chances are, you won't need to adjust this at all.

For sleeve length, things get slightly more complicated. You should measure the favorite sweater on the inside of the sleeve, from the armpit down to the bottom of the cuff.

If you are knitting a *drop-sleeve sweater* (the sleeve attaches flush to the body of the sweater and there is no cap shaping), this measurement should match the entire length of the sleeve. If it doesn't, make your adjustment

along the length of the sleeve, after the cuff. If the sleeve needs to be shorter, stop knitting or crocheting when the sleeve is the right length. If that means you miss one or two increase rows, don't sweat it.

If you are making a *raglan sleeve sweater* (the front and back of the sweater are angled inward and the top of the sleeve is correspondingly angled inward), you'll make your adjustment after the cuff, but before the part where you (usually) are instructed to bind off about an inch of stitches and begin decreasing toward the shoulder. First figure out how many rows of knitting you're trying to get rid of or add by multiplying your rows-per-inch gauge (you wouldn't *dream* of making a sweater without first making a gauge swatch, right?) by the length you are trying to decrease or increase your sleeve. For example, if you're trying to make your sleeves an inch shorter and your gauge is 6 rows per inch, you need to get rid of 6 rows, and if you're making it an inch longer, you need to add 6 rows. Where will you adjust those rows? You'll simply add or subtract them as evenly as you can between

DROP SLEEVE

adjust sweater length here

adjust sleeve length here

RAGLAN SLEEVE

adjust sweater length here

adjust sleeve length here

SET-IN SLEEVE

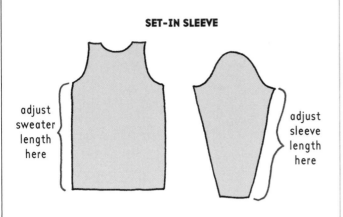

adjust sweater length here

adjust sleeve length here

your increase rows. So, if you're trying to subtract 6 rows, and your pattern says to increase 1 stitch each side of your sleeve every 4th row 8 times, just increase 1 stitch each side every 3rd row 6 times instead, and continue with the "every fourth row" directions for the last two increases. You'll have ditched 6 rows that way, and your sleeve will be 1" shorter, just like you want. Similarly, to make the sleeves a bit longer, add those rows in between the increase rows (in the example above, you'd increase 1 stitch each side every 5th row 6 times, then continue the pattern as written). The same rule applies for a *set-in sleeve* (cap-shaped): Make your lengthening or shortening before you get to the shaping for the top of the sleeve.

Don't sweat this too hard: It's not terribly difficult to lengthen a sweater or sleeves after the fact by simply unraveling the cast-on and any cuff or bottom-edge ribbing, then knitting in the opposite direction for an inch or so, and reknitting the cuff. (Don't forget, however, that this technique will not succeed if you're working a cabled or knit-and-purl pattern—or you'll

end up with a Frankensweater, the way I did.) Besides, unless your man is King Kong, usually the sleeve length will turn out to be fine as written. And heck, he can always roll the cuffs up a bit, just like he does his shirtsleeves.

A Lighter Shade of Pale
Choosing Colors

Selecting the appropriate color for a man couldn't be easier: Ask him. As I explained earlier, most men have a color palette that they stick to, and they stick to it religiously. Even if he's a "summer" but wears only "winter" colors, for god's sake, make him the sweater in a color he likes. I've heard it suggested that you take your man with you to the yarn store to pick out his own yarn for the project, but this might backfire for two reasons. For one, it involves taking your man into a yarn store, which, unless he's also a knitter (in which case he can make his own dang sweater), he is not likely to enjoy. For another, he might choose a yarn that is totally inappropriate for the project you are making him—such as a bulky cotton for a worsted-weight cardigan, which would not only require that you recalculate every single stitch of the pattern but would also mean, given the weight of cotton, that the cardigan would reach his knees before long. Better to ask him what colors he wants his sweater in and choose a suitable yarn yourself. Or, if it's going to be a surprise, just observe him in his natural habitat. If he likes to wear green, make him something green; if he wears a lot of blue, make him something blue. And for crying out loud, don't ask him what his "favorite color" is, under the guise of getting to know him better. His favorite color may very well be purple, even though all he ever wears is gray and black. He might even think you're planning on buying him a car or a motorcycle, and boy won't that be a disappointment when you hand him a purple hand-knit hat. So go by his wardrobe and you'll be sure to make the right color choice. And remember that "black" doesn't have to mean boring, flat-out black; a tweedy charcoal, or a black with flecks of other colors, or something striped with other shades he likes to wear—tan, brown, and white, for instance—would also fit the bill.

There's one exception to the make-what-he-wears rule when it comes to colors, and that is if you are making a project for the kind of guy who's really into something that has a specific set of colors associated with it, like his alma mater. Make something in your man's favorite team colors and you'll probably end up with a winner, especially if what you're making is sporty in style to begin with. Red and white socks or a red and white pullover will please any Red Sox fan, as will a navy blue and white hoodie for that Yalie in your life. Just be sure you get the right shade: Harvard's crimson is not the same as red, and the Green Bay Packers don't wear chartreuse. Even a man's ethnic background or affinity can yield successful color

Not Your Average Joe A few years ago, my husband and I were fortunate to adopt a son. Despite being all boy, he has demonstrated his appreciation of my knitting by requesting that I knit sweaters and accessories for his G.I. Joes—all six of them. As the mom of a boy who believes all the Joes deserve to be outfitted in hand-knit sweaters, and if at all possible a knit tent for them would be just great too, you can imagine my immense joy upon discovering camouflage-colored yarn. Despite the fact that this yarn is neither expensive nor luxurious, I'm certain of this: The one who will always be my little boy will be happy! Linda Ball, Easton, PA

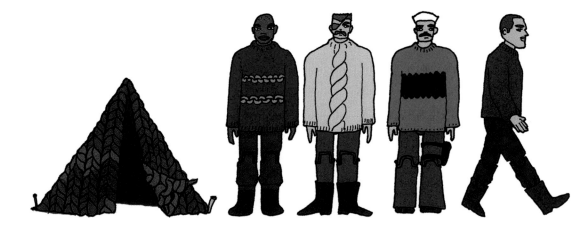

combos: Green, red, and white might be just the thing for your Italian stallion, and a sweater or hat in black, red, yellow, and green would be embraced by many a Reggae fan.

Hair of the dog
Choosing the Right Fiber

If you're concerned that your man's conservative clothing style means you're in for a major knitting or crocheting snoozefest, take heart: When it comes to fiber, you can sneak in a little something extra to sweeten your experience. While they don't often admit it, most men like a little luxury in their clothes, as the recent popularity of men's cashmere sweaters attests. *Seinfeld*'s George Costanza once admitted memorably that, if it were socially acceptable, he'd drape himself in velvet, and with a knit or crocheted item it is completely acceptable to drape your man in the finest of fibers. You might want to steer clear of fluffy angora or mohair, but alpaca, silk, cashmere, and camel are all fair game, as are actual game, such as buffalo hair or possum fur. Scan your local yarn store (LYS) or yarn catalog for exotic fiber blends, and, if you can afford it, use them with abandon in your men's projects. They might cost a little more, but he's worth it.

The Power of Example About twenty years ago, my college roommate and I decided we'd each knit a sweater for our respective boyfriends for Christmas. Whenever her boyfriend came over, she'd hide her knitting, while I'd sit on the couch, knitting openly, and she'd say things like what a wonderful girlfriend I was for knitting my man such a beautiful sweater. Then, when my boyfriend came over, my knitting would go away, my roommate would sit on the couch knitting her boyfriend's sweater, and we'd talk about what a labor of love it was for her, and so on. When Christmas came, we gave our guys their respective sweaters, and they were sufficiently appreciative. My roommate and I both ended up marrying our sweater sweethearts, and are still married today. Betsey Beacon, North Haven, CT

Even the most rugged men prefer something soft against their skin, so merino wool is always a good choice. Cotton, while super-soft and a familiar favorite to most T-shirt wearing guys, is not always the best selection for knit menswear, because it weighs more and has less resilience than an animal-based fiber. But any nice cotton-blend yarn would work well for most of the projects in this book, especially if it's for someone who lives in a milder climate. And while Icelandic wool is a traditional choice for men's sweaters because it's as long wearing and hardy as steel wool, unfortunately, it can also feel like a pot scrubber against his skin. Instead, find something that looks just as macho but is secretly soft, such as a thick alpaca-and-wool blend. And there's one more way to keep him from being part of the *Itchy and Scratchy Show,* courtesy of a knitter I know: Launder your finished project in Eucalan (a no-rinse knit wash with lanolin), which makes all yarn feel as soft as cashmere. In the end, the best thing to do is test the yarn yourself. Hold it next to your cheek to see if it's soft enough for your man, and unless it's intended for a project that will always be worn over something else, like a cardigan, choose a fiber you know he wouldn't mind wearing next to his skin—something that might even make him feel just a bit pampered.

There are some other fibers you might want to consider using when knitting for a guy, especially if he is laundry-challenged: Try "superwash" sock yarn if you're making socks because it means he can machine-wash them. They'll need to be run through the gentle cycle and dried on low, but really, the fiber is nothing short of miraculous. And you aren't limited to yarn for socks alone; many other weights are also available in superwash—including super-soft worsted-weight fibers such as merino. There is still another option, although I'll warn all you yarn snobs to cover your eyes right now: Use an acrylic yarn, which is made to be machine washable, for a boy project, especially if he has a tendency to get dirty. Acrylic yarns, while not scratchy, can be downright squeaky, so do the cheek test to be sure what you're choosing is soft enough for your man's sensitive skin. Also, know that acrylic yarn has a tendency to pill, so advise your dude against washing it too much, because, over time, it will definitely be worse for the wear.

Unfortunately, some of the softest and most comfortable yarns are also the most difficult to launder. And you definitely don't want to have the sweater you've spent so much time on carelessly thrown into the washing machine and shrunk down to the size of a dog sweater. You know the saying, "Give a man a fish, he'll eat for a day. Teach a man to fish, he'll eat for a lifetime." Well, this is your chance to teach a man, not

Hey, Man! How to Wash a Hand-Knit

his item is made of _____. You won't need to wash it very often, but when it's time, please don't throw it in the washing machine. Instead, do this:

1. Fill a sink with lukewarm water, pour in a capful of mild dishwashing soap or baby shampoo, drop it in and gently squeeze the suds through it.

2. Let it soak for about five minutes.

3. Drain the sink, refill with cool water, and gently swish it around to get all the suds out. If it still seems sudsy, repeat this step.

4. Carefully squeeze most of the water out—don't wring it—then roll it up in a thick towel to get more water out.

5. Finally, lay it flat on a dry towel for a day or two. If there's a sweater-drying rack or a clean screen that can be balanced across two chairs, lay it flat on there and it'll dry a lot faster.

Don't worry, this isn't a job for Superman, and you can do it in the time it takes to wait for your pizza to be delivered. Take good care of this hand-knit and it will take good care of you for years to come.

Don't Ask, Don't Tell During my senior year of college, I knit my boyfriend a sampler afghan. It was huge and really lovely, made of bits of everything—popcorns, cables, you name it. We split up after the summer, but he kept the afghan. Twenty years later I met him again at our high school reunion; I asked him about the afghan, thinking maybe I could get it back. He shushed me, took me aside briefly, and said, "She thinks my mother made it." Shirley Warren, New Paltz, NY

how to fish, but how to hand wash if he wants a sweater to last a lifetime. Though things like hats, scarves, and mittens need to be washed at most once a year and sweaters that are worn over clothes, only rarely, eventually, most hand-knit items will need to get cleaned. And that usually means hand washing them. So I suggest giving a bottle of no-rinse soap along with your gift and a tag with the simple directions on page 19, so that your recipient knows exactly what to do.

All in all, there's no reason you can't succeed in stitching something that a man will wear—in fact, women (and men) have been doing it for more than 800 years. Just pay special attention to fit, color, and fiber, and he'll be likely to wear it for a long, long time. If you can, get your guy involved in the process. Ask him which projects he likes in this book, and remind him that you can make anything he likes in whatever color he would prefer—help him see past the exact sweater in the photograph and imagine something customized just for him. Take measurements from a favorite article of clothing, and adjust the pattern, if necessary, so it fits him to a T. Splurge on the best fiber your budget will allow, paying special attention to color, softness, and washability of the yarn you choose.

If after all of that, he still won't wear it—well, instead of catching a resentment, just take it back and find someone who would appreciate it, such as a family member or a colleague. Try selling it online, like on eBay or Etsy, for instance, or donating it to a charity (there's almost always a soldier somewhere who would appreciate something handmade). Or wear it yourself for that special boyfriend-sweater look.

Most of all, have fun. Because in the end, the joy of making a hand-stitched project isn't just in the product, it's in the process. Enjoy your time stitching, learn from it, perfect your skills, and relax your mind. And, as always, knit on!

Let's Hear it for the boys Male Designers Speak Up About
What It Takes to Make It in a Man's World (of Knit and Crochet)

"Men and women basically have the same needs and wants when it comes to handmade clothes," says Kellen Wallis, who designed the crocheted "Lidsville" cap in this book. "They want it to be customized for them, so that it fits perfectly, looks great, and is just what they were thinking about. Communication is the key. As for the pattern, I prefer to stick with something that's not fancy—just basic stitches all the way through, with maybe a few color changes." That doesn't mean the project has to be boring, however. "It's important to consider the man's age and interests. For instance, right now I'm working on a beanie with the Clash logo on it, and just about anything with a good-looking skull design on it will get me every time."

Peter Franzi, who designed the crocheted "Gatsby" sweater, agrees. "I'm sorry to say (and not wishing to offend anyone) that most of the crocheted clothing for men that's currently available reflects the taste of the woman designing or making it—not of the men themselves. I personally would not wear 95 percent of what is passed off as men's designs."

"I do not speak for all men," Franzi stresses, "but from my experience as a designer and from listening to and observing other men. First, no fancy embellishments or do-dads. Aran stitches are fine, but, for many, that is also too much. Second, stay away from anything high or tight on the neck. And work with muted colors or earth tones."

For Jared Flood, who designed "Smokin'," "the most important thing to guys is not to stand out too much in their sweater." Pay attention to sweater construction, he advises. "Guys like the fit of raglan, set-in, and saddle sleeves." Finally, he stresses the importance of color: "Earth tones, grays, and more muted colors are a safe bet, whereas self-striping and anything novelty is an immediate red light."

Drew Steinbrecher, who designed the "Ernie" sweater, would agree. "Choose something on the simple side," he says. "Men, for the most part, aren't that adventurous." And, he advises, "If you aren't sure about a sweater, a scarf or hat would be a better choice for guys."

PART II
the patterns

pattern recognition
How to Follow a Pattern

These patterns are written as simply and uniformly as possible. The abbreviations used in them are listed on the opposite page; any abbreviations that are particular to a certain pattern will be clearly noted at the beginning of its directions.

On the first page of each pattern there is a sidebar with the sizes and finished measurements of the project. Next you'll find a list of the materials used in the photographed designs, from brands and amounts of yarn to sizes and types of needles to other notions that are necessary.

Finally (and most important), there is information about gauge or how many stitches and how many rows will make a 4"/10cm swatch. Gauge is a vital part of any pattern but particularly the ones in this book—if your gauge is off, your project is not going to come out the right size. And if the sweater doesn't fit "just so," your guy probably won't wear it. To check your gauge, cast on (or chain up) a few more stitches than are needed for a 4" swatch, knit or crochet a couple of inches of fabric in the stitch pattern specified, and measure how many stitches and how many rows you get. Measure your swatch in a few places, and if you come up with different numbers, average them. If you're getting fewer stitches than you should, go down a needle or hook size and try again. If you're getting more stitches, go up a needle or hook size and re-knit. Keep on keepin' on until you find the needle size that makes your gauge *just* right.

If there is anything different or special about the pattern (like a particular kind of stitch or a note about how the project is constructed), it will be clearly indicated before the directions begin. After that, the directions are written in exactly the order you should knit or crochet. Once you figure out the size you are making, follow the directions for THAT SIZE ONLY. Sizes begin with the smallest size outside the parentheses and continue in ascending order inside the parentheses, like so: S (M, L, XL, XXL). A good tip is to circle the specific directions for the size you are making throughout.

The charts, pictures, diagrams, and schematics all serve to help you better understand how to construct your project. Continue to compare your piece to the pictures to ensure it is coming out correctly.

The patterns range in difficulty from those that are easy and straightforward to those that involve complex stitch patterns or color work. I haven't graded them "easy" or "hard," however, because I don't believe in it—I think there's no greater motivation to learn a new skill than a project that you really, truly want to make. If you can knit or crochet, you can make any of the projects in this book—it just might take a new stitcher a little longer to finish up than a seasoned one.

All the patterns were carefully vetted and technically edited. However, occasionally, errors do pop up. If you come across something in a pattern that just doesn't add up, check the errata page on my website: www.knithappens.com. Most important, enjoy yourself! If you follow the suggestions in the first chapter, your finished project is sure to be a hit. Knit (and crochet) on!

Knit and Crochet Abbreviations

Approx	Approximately
Beg	Begin(ning)(s)
BO	Bind off
CC	Contrasting color
Ch	Chain
Cn	Cable needle
CO	Cast on
Cont	Continue
Dc	Double crochet
Dec	Decrease
Dpn(s)	Double-pointed needle(s)
Ea	Each
Est	Establish(ed)(es)
Foll	Follow(ed)(ing)(s)
Hdc	Half-double crochet
Inc	Increase
K	Knit
Kfb	Knit in front and back of st
Kwise	Knitwise
LH	Left hand
Lp(s)	Loop(s)
M1	Make 1: *Pick up bar between sts and k tbl*
MC	Main color

Meas	Measure(s)
P	Purl
Patt(s)	Pattern(s)
Pfb	Purl in front and back of st
Pm	Place marker
PU	Pick up
Pwise	Purlwise
Rem(s)	Remain(s)(ing)
Rep	Repeat
Rev St st	Reverse stockinette st: *P on RS, k on WS*
RH	Right hand
Rm	Remove marker
Rnd(s)	Round(s)
RS	Right side
Sc	Single crochet
Sc2tog	Single crochet 2 together: *[Insert hook in next st and pull up a lp] twice, yo and pull through all 3 lps on hook.*
Sk2p	Slip, k2tog, psso: *Slip next st knitwise, k2tog, pass the slipped st over k2tog st.*
Skp	Slip, knit, psso: *Slip next st knitwise, k next st, pass the slipped st over k st.*
Sl	Slip

Sl st	Slip stitch
Sm	Slip marker
Ssk	Slip, slip, knit: *[Slip next st knitwise] twice, insert LH needle into both slipped sts and k2tog tbl.*
Ssp	Slip, slip, purl: *[Slip next st knitwise] twice, slip sts back onto LH needle purlwise, p2tog tbl.*
St(s)	Stitch(es)
St st	Stockinette st: *K on RS, p on WS*
Tbl	Through back loop
Tog	Together
Tr	Treble crochet
W&T	Wrap and Turn: *Slip next st, bring yarn to other side, slip st back onto LH needle, turn work.*
WS	Wrong side
WW	Work Wrap: *Pick up wrap and work together with wrapped st.*
Wy	Waste yarn
Wyib	With yarn in back
Wyif	With yarn in front
Yo	Yarn over

CHELSEA FOWLER-BIONDOLILLO

Skull Isle Hat and Mittens

Size

Hat: S (M, L)

Finished circumference: 20 (21, 23)"

Mittens: S/M (L)

Finished length: 9½ (10)"

Materials

Dalegarn *Baby Ull* (100% superwash merino wool; 50g/180 yd)

MC: 2 skeins #090 black

CC: 1 skein #4018 red

Note: One skein of each color is enough for either hat or mittens; two skeins MC and one of CC make both.

US 1 (2.25mm) 16" circular needles or double-pointed needles (set of 5), or size needed to obtain gauge.

Stitch markers

Waste yarn

Gauge

36 sts and 40 rows = 4" in St st

This hat was designed for my friend Mark, who says skulls make everything better. It is knit with superwash wool—both warm and easy-care enough for your most laundry-challenged guy! Not only is this ensemble perfect for your favorite skater or punk rocker, it's also an excellent way to practice your mad Fair Isle skillz. Very sexy in black and red, as shown here, the set would be equally cool in a more subtle gray-and-white combo. The pattern rows are easily memorized, and they stop before the crown/mitten top so the advanced beginner can focus on one new technique at a time. Be sure to twist your nonworking yarn with your working yarn whenever you don't use it for more than 3 stitches—otherwise your guy might get his fingers tangled up in the floats.

Directions for Hat

With MC, CO 168 (180, 208) sts. Pm and join. Work in k2, p2 rib until piece meas 1½" from beg.

Rnd 1 With MC, knit, inc 2 (0, 2) sts evenly around—170 (180, 210) sts.

Rnds 2–9 Work 8 rnds of Chart A.

Rnd 10 With MC, knit.

Rnds 11–15 Work 5 rnds of Chart B.

Rnd 16 With MC, knit.

Rnds 17–31 Work 15 rnds of Chart C.

Rnd 32 With MC, knit.

Rnds 33–37 Work 5 rnds of Chart B.

Break off CC and cont with MC only.

Work even in St st until hat meas 6½ (7½, 8)" from beg.

Crown Shaping

Rnd 1 *K8, k2tog; rep from * around—153 (162, 189) sts.

Rnds 2, 4, 6, 8 and 10 Knit.

Rnd 3 *K7, k2tog; rep from * around—136 (144, 168) sts.

Rnd 5 *K6, k2tog; rep from * around—119 (126, 147) sts.

Rnd 7 *K5, k2tog; rep from * around—102 (108, 126) sts.

Rnd 9 *K4, k2tog; rep from * around—85 (90, 105) sts.

Rnd 11 *K3, k2tog; rep from * around—68 (72, 84) sts.

Rnd 12 *K2, k2tog; rep from * around—51 (54, 63) sts.

Rnd 13 *K1, k2tog; rep from * around—34 (36, 42) sts.

Rnd 14 *K2tog; rep from * around—17 (18, 21) sts.

Rnd 15 K1 (0, 1), *k2tog; rep from * around—9 (9, 11) sts.

FINISHING

Break yarn, leaving a 6" tail. Thread tail through rem sts twice, pull snugly to close opening, and weave in end securely.

Directions for Mittens

With MC, CO 72 (80) sts. Pm and join. Work in St st for ¾".

Join CC and work in two-color rib as foll:

Rnd 1 *K2 MC, p2 CC; rep from * around.

Rep rnd 1 for 2".

Break off CC and cont in MC only.

K 1 rnd, p 3 rnds.

Thumb Gusset

Rnd 1 Kfb, pm, k to last 2 sts, pm, kfb, k1—5 gusset sts between markers.

Rnd 2 Knit.

Rnd 3 K to 1 st before next marker, kfb, sm, k to next marker, sm, kfb, k to end—2 gusset sts added.

Rep rnds 2 and 3 until there are 27 (31) gusset sts between markers—96 (108) sts.

Work even in St st until mitten meas 5¾ (6)" from beg.

Hand

Rnd 1 K to 1 st before next marker and place previous 26 (30) gusset sts onto wy. Remove gusset markers. CO 0 (2) sts, pm and join—70 (80) sts.

Rnds 2–4 Knit.

Rnds 5–9 Work 5 rnds of Chart B.

Rnd 10 With MC, knit.

Rnds 11–25 Work 15 rnds of Chart C.

Rnd 26 With MC, knit.

Rnds 27–31 Work 5 rnds of Chart B.

Break off CC and cont in MC only.

Work even in St st until mitten meas 8¾ (9)" from beg.

Shape Tip

Size S/M only:

Rnd 1 [K15, k2tog, k16, k2tog] twice—66 sts.

Rnd 2 Knit.

Rnd 3 [K14, k2tog, k15, k2tog] twice—62 sts.

Rnd 4 Knit.

Cont dec 4 sts every other row, working 1 fewer st before each dec, until 42 sts rem. Then dec every row until 6 sts rem.

Size L only:

Rnd 1 [K18, k2tog] 4 times—76 sts.

Rnd 2 Knit.

Rnd 3 [K17, k2tog] 4 times—72 sts.

Rnd 4 Knit.

Cont dec 4 sts every other row, working 1 fewer st before each dec, until 52 sts rem. Then dec every row until 8 sts rem.

All sizes:

Break yarn, leaving a 6" tail. Thread tail through rem sts twice, pull snugly and weave in end securely.

Thumb

Distribute 26 (30) thumb sts evenly over 3 or 4 dpns. With MC, PU and k1 (3) sts across gap—27 (33) sts. Pm and join.

Work even in St st for 1½ (2)".

Shape Tip

Rnd 1 [K7 (9), k2tog] 3 times—24 (30) sts.

Rnd 2 Knit.

Rnd 3 [K6 (8), k2tog] 3 times—21 (27) sts.

Rnd 4 Knit.

Cont dec 3 sts every other rnd, working 1 fewer st before dec, until 12 (18) sts rem. Then dec every rnd until 9 sts rem.

Last rnd K1, *k2tog; rep from * around—5 sts.

Break yarn, leaving a 6" tail. Thread tail through rem sts twice, pull snugly and weave in end securely.

FINISHING

Weave in ends.

About Chelsea I learned to knit after going to my first wool festival in Taos, NM. Since then, I've knit countless pairs of socks, a few ill-fitting sweaters, a multitude of scarves, and some beautiful lace. At my last wool fest in Rhinebeck, NY, I bought my first spinning wheel and (with two good friends) filled the back of a VW "Beetle" with roving to spin. I don't spin much now that I live in Austin, TX, where I work as an IT project manager, but knitting and knitters are too much fun to quit over a few 100° days. Every now and then I update my blog, "small hands," thedevashands.blogspot.com.

Chart A

5 sts

Chart B

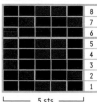

5 sts

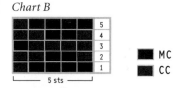

■ MC
■ CC

Chart C

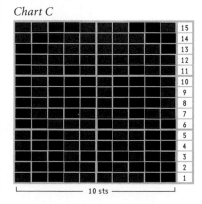

10 sts

KELLEN WALLIS

Lidsville

I bought a cap like this in a store, and was inspired to try and make a similar crocheted version. I had never designed anything before and just went for it, and with some experimenting I eventually got what you see in this pattern. I love this hat because in one day it's possible to see a punk, rude boy, rapper, or pop princess wearing this style of cap. Also, if you're good at charting images, the top piece would be a great place for a picture. In fact, the whole cap can be customized to suit your man's style.

Directions

Note: Ch 1 does not count as first stitch. Adjust hook size for smaller or larger size hats.

BACK (MAKE 4)
Ch 9.

Row 1 Sc in 2nd ch from hook, sc in each ch across, turn—8 sc.

Rows 2–8 Ch 1, sc in each st across, turn—8 sc.

Row 9 Ch 1, 2 sc in first st, sc in each st to last st, 2 sc in last st, turn—10 sc.

Rows 10–17 Ch 1, sc in each st across, turn—10 sc.

Rows 18, 20 and 22 Ch 1, sc2tog, sc in each st to last 2 sts, sc2tog, turn—4 sc after row 22.

Rows 19, 21 and 23 Ch 1, sc in each st across, turn.

Size
Finished circumference: 23"

Materials
Tahki *Donegal Tweed Homespun* (100% wool; 100g/18 yd), 2 skeins #894

I/9 (5.5mm) crochet hook, or size needed to obtain gauge

Plastic canvas

Gauge
7 sts and 8 rows = 2" in single crochet

*Brim template,
actual size*

Row 24 Ch 1, sc2tog twice, turn—2 sc.

Row 25 Ch 1, sc in each st across, turn.

Row 26 Ch 1, sc2tog, turn—1 sc.

Row 27 Ch 1, sc in next st.

Fasten off.

TOP
Ch 39.

Row 1 Sc in 2nd ch from hook, sc in each ch across, turn—38 sc.

Rows 2–5 Ch 1, sc in each st across, turn—38 sc.

Row 6 Ch 1, sc2tog, sc in each st to last 2 sts, sc2tog, turn—36 sc.

Row 7 Ch 1, sc in each st across, turn.

Rows 8–25 Rep rows 6 and 7—18 sc after row 25.

Row 26 Ch 1, sc2tog twice, sc in each st to last 4 sts, sc2tog twice, turn—14 sc.

Fasten off.

SIDE (MAKE 2)
Ch 9.

Row 1 Sc in 2nd ch from hook, sc in each ch across, turn—8 sc.

Rows 2–5 Ch 1, sc in each st across, turn—8 sc.

Row 6 Ch 1, sc2tog, sc in each st across, turn—7 sc.

Rows 7–8 Ch 1, sc in each st across, turn.

Row 9 Ch 1, sc in each st to last 2 sts, sc2tog, turn—6 sc.

Rows 10–11 Ch 1, sc in each st across, turn.

Row 12 Ch 1, sc2tog, sc in each st across, turn—5 sc.

Rows 13–14 Ch 1, sc in each st across, turn.

Row 15 Ch 1, sc in each st to last 2 sts, sc2tog, turn—4 sc.

Rows 16–17 Ch 1, sc in each st across, turn.

Row 18 Ch 1, sc2tog, sc in each st across, turn—3 sc.

Rows 19–20 Ch 1, sc in each st across, turn.

Row 21 Ch 1, sc in next st, sc2tog, turn—2 sc.

Rows 22–23 Ch 1, sc in each st across, turn.

Row 24 Ch 1, sc2tog, turn—1 sc.

Rows 25–26 Ch 1, sc in next st, turn.

Fasten off.

BRIM
Ch 3.

Row 1 Sc in 2nd ch from hook, sc in next ch, turn—2 sc.

Row 2 Ch 1, 2 sc in each st across, turn—4 sc.

Rows 3, 5, 7, 9, 11, 13 and 15 Ch 1, sc in each st across, turn.

Row 4 Ch 1, sc in next st, 2 sc in next 2 sts, sc in each st across, turn—6 sc.

Row 6 Ch 1, sc in next 2 sts, 2 sc in next 2 sts, sc in each st across, turn—8 sc.

Row 8 Ch 1, sc in next 3 sts, 2 sc in next 2 sts, sc in each st across, turn—10 sc.

Row 10 Ch 1, sc in next 4 sts, 2 sc in next 2 sts, sc in each st across, turn—12 sc.

Row 12 Ch 1, sc in next 5 sts, 2 sc in next 2 sts, sc in each st across, turn—14 sc.

Row 14 Ch 1, sc in next 6 sts, 2 sc in next 2 sts, sc in each st across, turn—16 sc.

Rows 16–24 Ch 1, sc in each st across, turn.

Row 25 Ch 1, sc in next 6 sts, sc2tog twice, sc in each st across, turn—14 sc.

Rows 26, 28, 30, 32, 34 and 36 Ch 1, sc in each st across, turn.

Row 27 Ch 1, sc in next 5 sts, sc2tog twice, sc in each st across, turn—12 sc.

Row 29 Ch 1, sc in next 4 sts, sc2tog twice, sc in each st across, turn—10 sc.

Row 31 Ch 1, sc in next 3 sts, sc2tog twice, sc in each st across, turn—8 sc.

Row 33 Ch 1, sc in next 2 sts, sc2tog twice, sc in each st across, turn—6 sc.

Row 35 Ch 1, sc in next st, sc2tog twice, sc in each st across, turn—4 sc.

Row 37 Ch 1, sc2tog twice, turn—2 sc.

Row 38 Ch 1, sc in each st across—2 sc.

Fasten off.

BUTTON

Ch 2.

Row 1 6 sc in 2nd ch from hook, sl st in first sc to join—6 sc.

Row 2 Ch 1, 2 sc in each st around, sl st in first sc to join—12 sc.

Row 3 Ch 1, sc2tog 6 times, sl st in first sc to join—6 sc.

Row 4 Ch 1, sc in each st around, sl st in first sc to join—6 sc.

Fasten off, leaving a long tail.

INNER BAND

Ch 5.

Row 1 Sc in 2nd ch from hook, sc in each st across, turn—4 sc.

Rows 2–74 Ch 1, sc in each st across, turn.

Fasten off.

Assembly

BODY

Join pieces using sl st with RS together. Join the 4 back pieces with foundation ch at bottom and points at top. Working from row 9 to row 9 of assembled back, join the top piece across top of back piece. Working from row 1 to row 8 of assembled back, join foundation ch edge of side piece, then join side of side piece to side of top, ending on last row of top edge to top.

BRIM

Using template, cut brim support out of plastic canvas and insert it into brim. Enclose using sl st.

Turn hat inside out and sl st brim to hat, keeping close to edge of brim.

INNER BAND

Fit inside lower edge of hat. Starting at the back, sc hat to headband, skipping every other st of hat, working every st across brim, then skipping every other st of hat to end. Fasten off. Sew ends of band together.

FINISHING

Slip beg tail through to WS of button tog with end tail. Using tails, sew to top of cap where 4 points of back pieces meet. Weave in ends.

About Kellen I started crocheting to make a scarf for my girlfriend, Violet, inspired by my friend Scott who was crocheting a whole blanket at the time. I progressed to making some beanie-style hats, which completely threw me for a loop for months, until one day it clicked. I've been making beanies, sweaters, and charts for them for a couple years now. I live in a yarn-filled apartment in northern California with my amazing knitter girlfriend.

LINDSAY HENRICKS

Uncle Argyle Scarves

This scarf will work for any guy of any age. One of the most fun things about making it is picking out the color combos—I spent way too much time standing in front of a wall of yarn choosing colors for these two. For the first one, I used my favorite purple shade of yarn because it always reminds me of Prince and paired it with brown for a subtle, sophisticated pattern. In the second, I paired that same brown with a green heather for a bolder, more modern look. The scarf is knit using the double knitting technique, which makes it reversible without stranding, curling, or other problems you tend to run into when working with two colors.

Special technique
DOUBLE KNITTING

Double knitting creates a reversible double thickness of fabric, where the color work on one side is the exact opposite of the color work on the other side. When working double knitting, you will be holding two colors of yarn at all times. The first stitch of a row/round will always be a knit stitch using one color, followed by a purl stitch using the opposite color. You will continue alternating knit and purl stitches across the row/round, always bringing BOTH yarns to the back of your work before making a knit stitch, and BOTH yarns to the front of your work before making a purl stitch. When working back and forth in rows, make sure to TWIST colors together before starting each row. *Note:* When following a double knitting chart, each box in the chart represents two stitches. Refer to the chart key for further directions.

Size

Finished width: 7"

Finished length: 64"

Materials

Cascade Yarns *Cascade 220* (100% wool; 100g/220 yd)

Purple scarf:

2 hanks #2403 (MC)

2 hanks #2421 (CC)

Green scarf:

2 hanks #2403 (MC)

2 hanks #9461 (CC)

US 7 (4.5mm) straight needles

Gauge

16 sts and 22 rows = 4" in double knit st

About Lindsay I learned to knit while I was home for the summer after my first year of college. After walking into the local yarn shop, I was instantly hooked. I learned the backward loop cast-on and knit stitch from my mom, and taught myself more techniques from books. After I graduated in 2005, I started working at the Celtic Knot Yarn Shop in Ellicott City, MD. My coworkers have been so generous and supportive, and they've encouraged me to try things I never would have done otherwise (like submitting patterns for publication). Thank goodness my husband suggested I check to see if they were hiring!

Odd-numbered rows
- ▨ K1 MC, P1 CC
- ▨ K1 CC, P1 MC

Even-numbered rows
- ▨ K1 CC, P1 MC
- ▨ K1 MC, P1 CC

Directions

With MC, CO 58 sts.

Foundation row (WS) [K1 MC, p1 CC] 29 times.

Work 14 rows of chart 23 times.

Work row 1 of chart once more to complete argyle pattern.

Next row Rep foundation row.

Last row With MC only, *k1, p1; rep from * across.

BO row With MC only, k1, *p2tog, pass 1st st over 2nd st (1 st on RH needle); rep from * to last st, p1, pass 1st st over 2nd st. Break yarn and pull through last st.

Weave in ends.

NIENKE PAAP

Celtic Beanie

I designed this beanie as a gift for a male friend. Since he spends a lot of time outdoors, I used a double knitting technique, the two layers making it extra warm even on a windy day. Double knitting also makes the garment reversible, creating a negative of the pattern on the inside. I drew up a Celtic knot, as I was obsessed with cables at the time, but for this hat I preferred working with colors. The result is a beanie that's kind of a fakeout—you get the look of cables, without any cabling! The color choice was easy, my friend being a real ecoconscious kind of guy, but I think that it would also look good in strongly contrasting colors.

Size

Finished circumference: 20"

Materials

Mission Falls *1824 Wool*
(100% wool; 50g/85 yd)

MC: 2 balls #018 Spruce

CC: 2 balls #028 Pistachio

US 8 (5mm) double-pointed needles
(set of 5), or size needed to obtain gauge.

8 stitch markers

Gauge

18 sts and 26 rows = 4" in St st

Special technique
DOUBLE KNITTING
See Uncle Argyle Scarves (page 36) for double knitting directions.

Double Knit
K3, P1 Rib Stitch
*[Hold both colors to back, k1 MC; hold both colors to front; p1 CC] 3 times, hold MC in front and CC in back, p1 MC, k1 CC; rep from * around.

Directions

With CC, loosely CO 76 sts. Pm and join.

Foundation rnd Join MC. *With both colors in back, k1 MC, do not slip st off needle; bring both colors to front and p1 CC in same st; slip st off needle; rep from * around—152 sts.

Work in Double Knit K3, P1 Rib St for 6 rnds with MC in front.

Work 2 rnds in Double Knit St st with MC in front.

Work 19 rnds of chart.

Work 7 more rnds in Double Knit St st with MC in front.

SHAPE CROWN

Next rnd *Pm, [k1 MC, p1 CC] 9 times, pm, [k1 MC, p1 CC] 10 times; rep from * 3 times more.

Dec rnd *Sm, sl 1 MC kwise, insert RH needle into next 2 sts (CC and MC) as if to k2tog and sl both to RH needle, then sl 1 CC st back to LH needle. Insert LH needle into 2 MC sts on RH needle and k2tog tbl MC, then p2tog CC. Double Knit St st to next marker; rep from * around—136 sts.

Rep dec rnd every rnd until 24 sts rem—12 sts each color.

Final rnd *K2tog MC, p2tog CC (as in dec rnd), k1 MC, p1 CC; rep from * 3 times more—8 sts.

FINISHING

Break yarns. Thread MC tail through MC sts and CC tail through CC sts with tapestry needle. Pull tight to close and sew to secure. Weave in ends.

About Nienke I learned to knit in the forests of Australia. Since then, I've knit in various locations, but my favorite stitching spot is high up in a tree, when I'm killing time, waiting for the police to come and arrest me, as I'm there trying to prevent the forest from being cut down. I very much believe in a DIY lifestyle and think that knitting forms a perfect addition to this. Currently I live in The Netherlands, where I spend most of my time on (eco)activism. You can see more of my work, as well as some of the places where I've knit, at www.willknitfortattoos.com.

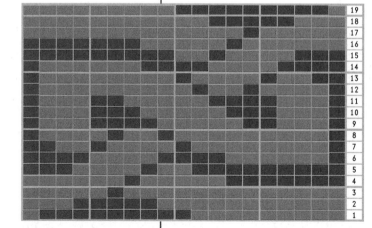

■ K1 MC, P1 CC
■ K1 CC, P1 MC

Size

Finished width: 5½"

Finished length: 51"

Materials

Louet Gems Sport Weight
(100% merino; 50g/ 112 yd)

MC: 2 skeins #21 Cloud Grey

CC: 2 skeins #49 Charcoal

US 5 (3.75mm) straight needles

Gauge

20 sts and 24 rows = 4" in double knit stitch

KIM HAMLIN

Brooklyn Bridge Scarf

Like many thousands of Brooklynites before me, I have made the journey in and out of Manhattan more times than I can count. While I'm thankful for a zippy subway system, there's something monumental about making the journey above ground by walking across the Brooklyn Bridge. The first time I did it, I stood beneath the huge stone pylons in awe. How many people had touched these stones? How many people had passed, just like me, on their way home, or had traveled the globe just to stand there? How many petticoats, spats, love beads, berets, down vests, or jeans had gone by? The inspiration for this scarf is easy to see: an awesome project to match one of the coolest places to be . . . ever. Best of all, done in double knit fabric, where the inverse of an image appears on the other side of the fabric, this scarf gives you two Brooklyn Bridges: the day view on one side, and the night view on the other.

Special technique
DOUBLE KNITTING
See Uncle Argyle Scarves (page 36) for double knitting directions.

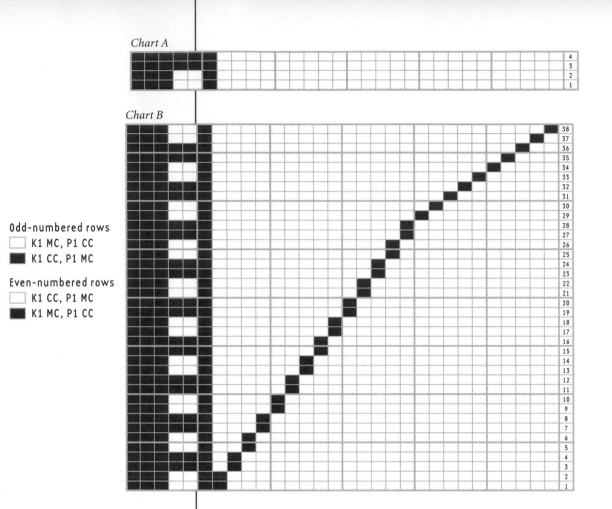

Chart A

Chart B

Odd-numbered rows
☐ K1 MC, P1 CC
■ K1 CC, P1 MC

Even-numbered rows
☐ K1 CC, P1 MC
■ K1 MC, P1 CC

Directions

With CC, CO 60 sts.

Working in double knitting, work charts as foll:

Chart A 13 times, Chart B once, Chart C once, Chart A 10 times, Chart B once, Chart C once, Chart A 13 times.

For a longer scarf, add an equal number of Chart A reps to every A section.

When all charts have been worked, BO with CC in k1, p1 rib.

FINISHING

Weave in ends. Block lightly.

Chart C

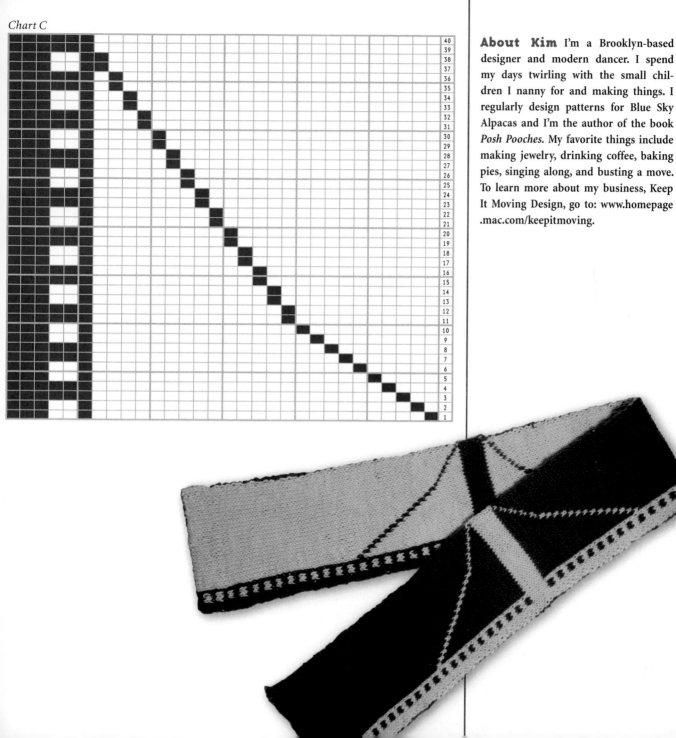

About Kim I'm a Brooklyn-based designer and modern dancer. I spend my days twirling with the small children I nanny for and making things. I regularly design patterns for Blue Sky Alpacas and I'm the author of the book *Posh Pooches*. My favorite things include making jewelry, drinking coffee, baking pies, singing along, and busting a move. To learn more about my business, Keep It Moving Design, go to: www.homepage .mac.com/keepitmoving.

DEBBIE STOLLER

Half-Pipe Hat

If a watch cap and a baseball cap had a baby, it would be this simple brimmed cap. And in the past year or so, it is this style of cap that seems to have become the winter headgear of choice for all types of men here in New York City—from skater boys to hip-hoppers, jocks to indie rockers, janitors to baristas. For sale everywhere at street-corner vendors as well as high-end hipster boutiques, the cap is almost always constructed just as it is in this pattern: as a standard, circular-knit tubelike cap, with decreasing at the crown, that's folded up at the bottom and has a C-shaped brim stuck in and stitched down. Of course, this Half-Pipe Hat is a few steps up from the rest, as it is made in luxuriously soft baby camel hair yarn. And since it requires only two balls of the stuff, it's an affordable extravagance. Half-Pipe Hat is a quick project and an easy gift for every man in your life.

Special technique
TUBULAR CAST-ON

Begin with a slip knot on your needle, leaving a very long tail. Hold the needle and yarn just as you would for the long-tail cast on, with the needle in your right hand and the yarn tail over the thumb of your left hand, the yarn ball end over your pointer finger, and both ends held in the lower fingers of your left hand. This cast-on is worked exclusively on the two inner strands.

Size

20" circumference

Materials

Classic Elite *Blithe* (100% baby camel; 25g/128 yd), 2 balls #60690 Charcoal

US 9 (5.5mm) straight needles

US 9 (5.5mm) 16" circular needle (optional)

US 9 (5.5mm) double-pointed needles (set of 5), or size needed to obtain gauge

Plastic canvas (10 holes per inch)

Gauge

18 sts and 24 rows = 4" in St st with 2 strands held tog

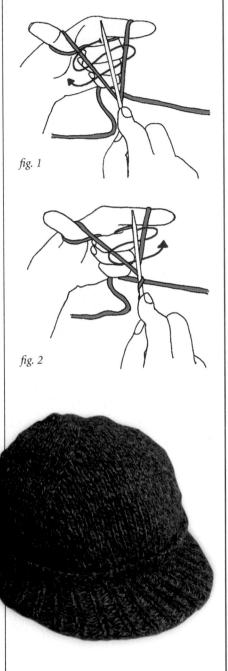

fig. 1

fig. 2

First stitch Turn the point of your needle counterclockwise to bring it over then under the strand on your thumb, bringing it up between the two strands. Then turn it clockwise to bring it over then under the strand on your pointer, bringing the loop you've just made on your needle under the strand on your thumb and snug with the previous st, so the thumb strand will secure the stitch (fig. 1).

Next stitch Do the same in reverse: Swing the point of your needle clockwise over and then under the strand on your pointer, and bring it up between the two strands. Then turn it counterclockwise over and then under the strand on your thumb, and bring the loop under the strand on your pointer, snug with the previous st, so the pointer strand will secure the stitch (fig. 2).

Continue making this "figure 8" in the air with the point of your needle, first making a stitch from the yarn over your thumb, then the next one from the yarn over your pointer, until all stitches are made. When all stitches have been cast on, tie the ball and tail ends together loosely. This tubular cast-on is perfect for the beginning of ribbing, as it is very stretchy.

Directions

Note: Pattern is worked using 2 strands tog throughout.

With 2 strands held tog, and using Tubular Cast-on, CO 80 sts onto straight needles.

Transfer sts to circular needle or dpns and work 1 row k1, p1 rib, beg with p1. Pm and join.

Cont in k1, p1 rib as est for 5".

Work in St st for 1".

SHAPE CROWN
Rnd 1 *K18, k2tog, pm; rep from * 3 times more—76 sts.

Rnd 2 Knit.

Rnd 3 *K to 2 sts before marker, k2tog; rep from * 3 times more—72 sts.

Rnd 4 Knit.

Rep rnds 3 and 4 eight times more, switching to dpns as necessary, then rep row 3 six times—16 sts.

Slip first 8 sts onto 1 dpn, and last 8 sts onto a 2nd dpn.
Graft sts together.

FINISHING

Following brim template, cut brim out of plastic mesh.

Fold ribbing up at 2½" point so beg and end of ribbing meet.

Fold hat in half and pm approx ½" in from outer corners of fold.

With corners of brim at marked points, pin ribbing in place to enclose brim, stretching rib to keep 1" at beg and end of ribbing free. Using running stitch, sew brim in place.

Weave in ends.

Brim template, actual size

Size

Finished width: 5"

Finished length: 65"

Materials

Blue Sky Alpacas *Dyed Cotton* (100% cotton; 100g/150 yd), 3 hanks #623 Toffee

US 8 (5mm) straight needles

Cable needle

Gauge:

29 sts = 4" in patt st

MICAH P. DAMMEYER

Antlers Scarf

One day I realized that, aside from my first knitting project, I had yet to knit a nice scarf for myself. I knew I couldn't sport something boring and be proud that I'd knit it, so I set up a bunch of cables and went to town: two on the sides and a larger one in the center. After a couple of repeats, it's pretty easy to memorize and take with you on the bus or train. I've knit a few Antlers Scarves now and can crank one out in a couple of Saturday afternoons of steady coffee drinking and marathon knitting—and I consider myself a slow knitter. It's a great project if you've never tried cables before and really want something to show off when you're done. And its rugged good looks mean it will look great whether worn on a boys-only fishing trip or to a fancy seafood restaurant.

About Micah My knitting addiction began at a family Christmas get-together. My brother and I were flipping through his wife's pattern books, saying, "This can't be any harder than tying trout flies or building houses—we can do this." Our mom cast on for us and we were off! Since then, knitting has kept me busy when the fish weren't biting, and introduced me to lots of whacky people and helped my brother and me become closer. Our other brother thinks we're crazy. I now live in a quiet neighborhood in Washington, D.C., where I paint and create after the 9-to-5 job. I do my best to get together with the weekly knitting group, but nothing's as relaxing as knitting through a nice Manhattan on the couch with the pooch.

Special abbreviations

C4B: Sl 2 to cn and hold in back, k2, k2 from cn.

C4F: Sl 2 to cn and hold in front, k2, k2 from cn.

C6B: Sl 3 to cn and hold in back, k3, k3 from cn.

C6F: Sl 3 to cn and hold in front, k3, k3 from cn.

Directions

CO 36 sts.

Foundation row (WS) Purl.

Row 1 K7, p1, k6, C4B, C4F, k6, p1, k7.

Rows 2, 4 and 6 P7, k1, p20, k1, p7.

Row 3 K7, p1, k4, C4B, k4, C4F, k4, p1, k7.

Row 5 K7, p1, k2, C4B, k8, C4F, k2, p1, k7.

Row 7 K1, C6B, p1, C4B, k12, C4F, p1, C6F, k1.

Row 8 Rep row 2.

Rep rows 1–8 until scarf meas approx 65" or desired length, ending with row 7. BO.

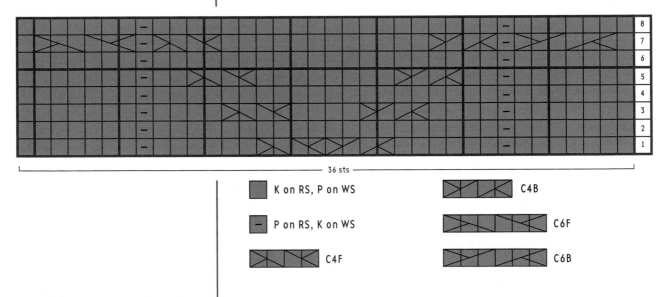

— 36 sts —

	K on RS, P on WS		C4B
	P on RS, K on WS		C6F
	C4F		C6B

Size

Finished circumference: 19" (will stretch to fit)

Finished length: 8½"

Materials

Rowan Classic *Cashsoft DK* (54% extra-fine merino, 33% acrylic microfiber, 10% cashmere; 50g/142 yd)

MC: 2 balls #513 Poison

CC: 1 ball #525 Kingfisher

US 3 (3.25mm) straight needles, or size needed to obtain gauge

5 stitch markers

Gauge

26 sts and 38 rows = 4" in garter rib

TERRA JAMIESON

Ski Beanie

Here in Halifax, Nova Scotia, the weather is extremely unpredictable. We often experience at least two seasons in one day! As a result, it's nice to have clothing that can serve under a variety of conditions. I designed this hat for my husband—I wanted to make a tuque that would keep his head warm, look stylish, and be comfortable enough to wear indoors during bad hair days. Made in a luscious cashmere blend, it's so soft and comfy that he rarely wants to take it off, no matter what the weather. The Ski Beanie is knit flat, in an easy-peasy garter rib with mirrored decreases, and seamed up the back.

Garter Rib Stitch

Multiple of 3 sts plus 2

Row 1 (RS) *K2, p1; rep from *, end k2.

Row 2 Purl.

Directions

With CC, CO 113 sts.

Row 1 (RS) *K1, p1; rep from *, end k1.

Row 2 *P1, k1; rep from *, end p1.

Change to MC and rep rows 1 and 2 once.

Cont with MC, work in Garter Rib Stitch until hat meas 5¾" from beg, ending with a WS row.

Next row (RS) Work in patt over next 12 sts, pm, [work in patt over next 22 sts, pm] 4 times, work in patt over next 13 sts.

Next row Purl.

Shape Crown

Row 1 (RS) [Work in patt to 2 sts before marker, k2tog, sm, ssk] 5 times, patt to end—103 sts.

Row 2 Purl.

Rows 3–18 Rep rows 1 and 2—23 sts after row 18.

Row 19 *K2tog; rep from *, end k1—12 sts.

FINISHING

Break yarn, leaving a 20" tail for sewing. Thread tail through rem sts and pull snug. With RS facing, sew seam, being careful to match row to row. Weave in ends.

About Terra I grew up in Nova Scotia and I am the granddaughter and great-granddaughter of knitters. Unfortunately, by the time I expressed an interest in learning the craft, my grandmother was suffering from arthritis and could no longer wield the needles. Armed with needles I inherited from my nan, I taught myself to knit from books and the Internet about five years ago. I have since developed an obsession with all things fiber related. When not knitting, I work in the field of water resources management and am finishing a Ph.D. in earth sciences. You can find me spinning, knitting, and harassing our golden retriever on my blog, slomoeknits.wordpress.com, or being noisy at our "Knitting Out Loud" group in downtown Halifax.

SHETHA NOLKE

Naughty/Nice Scarf

Even the mildest-mannered of men can be a bit of a cad at times, and this illusion scarf lets him hide his naughty side from the rest of the world. Looked at straight on, it's a basic striped scarf in a fiery red colorway. But hidden like a shadow among the flames are the silhouettes of two naked ladies, dancing on a pole that stretches from one end of the scarf to the other. Of course, these figures are revealed only when you look across the surface of the scarf, so when your guy is wearing the scarf, he'll see her every time he looks down. It's his little secret. But no worries—this lusty lady will make him think of no one but you.

Directions

Note: The scarf is worked in two halves from the bottom up. The two pieces are then joined with a seam at the back neck (center). When changing colors, run unused color along side of scarf, twisting together, being sure to keep tension even for smooth edges.

FIRST HALF

With MC, CO 42 sts (counts as row 1 of Chart 1).

Begin chart:

Row 2 Follow chart in MC.

Row 3 Purl in CC.

Row 4 Follow chart in CC.

Row 5 Purl in MC.

Size

Finished width: 6½"

Finished length: 69"

Materials

MC: Lorna's Laces *Shepherd Worsted* (100% wool; 100g/225 yd), 2 hanks #146 Flames

CC: Cascade Yarns *Cascade 220* (100% wool; 100g/220 yd), 2 hanks #8555 black

US 5 (3.75mm) straight needles, or size needed to obtain gauge

Spare needle for 3-needle BO

Stitch holder

Gauge

25 sts and 40 rows = 4" in chart pattern

Repeat rows 2–5 through row 342 of Chart 1, preceding each row from chart with a plain row of purl in same color.

SECOND HALF
Work same as first half following Chart 2.

FINISHING
To join the 2 halves, place sts of first half onto 2nd needle so needle points face the same direction with WS tog. Using CC, work 3-needle BO keeping width consistent with body of scarf. Weave in ends.

Chart 1

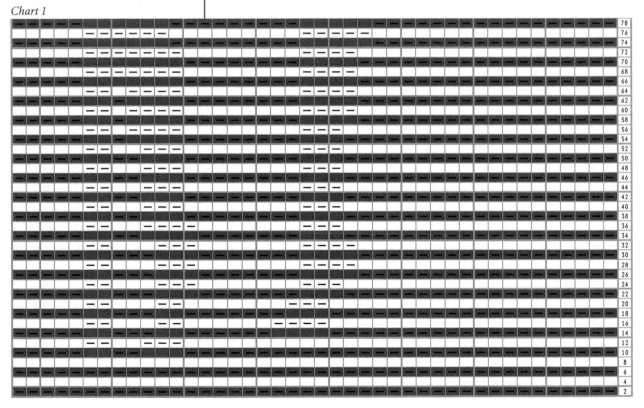

Note: Only even-numbered rows are shown. For odd-numbered rows, see directions.

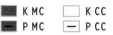

K MC ☐ K CC
P MC ⊟ P CC

Chart 1 contd.

Chart 1 contd.

Chart 2

Chart 2 contd.

Chart 2 contd.

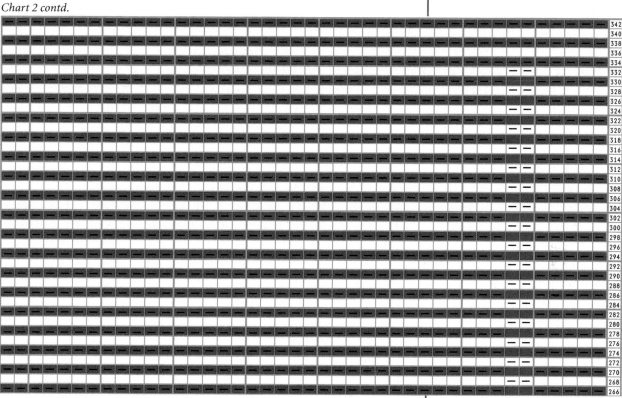

About Shetha Knitting has changed a lot for me over the last few years. Now that I've brought two little people into the world, my knitting projects have become very little, and quick to finish. Still, I occasionally enjoy delving into a deliciously impossible-seeming project just to prove to myself that I haven't lost my skillz. I delight in charting lace and cable patterns from written instructions. And when I really need a challenge, I reverse engineer an expensive garment I see online or in a store. One thing that never loses its fun and fascination is designing more and more interesting illusion patterns.

Size

One size (men's medium)

Finished length: 8½"

Finished circumference (at palm): 8½"

Materials

Rowan *Scottish Tweed DK* (100% wool; 50g/123 yd), 2 balls #029 Autumn

US 4 (3.5mm) circular needle (2)

US 6 (4mm) circular needle (2), or size needed to obtain gauge

Cable needle

Waste yarn

Stitch holders

Gauge

23 sts and 32 rows = 4" in reverse St st

KURT FAUSSET

Beer Gloves

These gloves are a modern reference to knitting's long-term relationship with fishermen. The "Whale Spine" cable that travels up the back of the hand is inspired by Matthew Barney's *Drawing Restraint 9*, a contemporary art-film piece about two occidental tourists who meet on the world's last working whaling ship. Since I threw back plenty of beers with fishermen in my hometown of Bradenton, FL, I added some seed stitching on the palm to help with cracking open a cold one.

Special technique

KNITTING IN THE ROUND ON TWO CIRCULAR NEEDLES

Cast all stitches onto one circ. Slip half of the sts onto the second circ. Slide all sts on *both* circs to the other ends of the needles. With the open side of the work facing you, take the needle with the first cast-on stitch in your left hand, and the other needle (with the ball-end of yarn) in your right. Join into a round by slipping the first st from your left needle onto the right, then lifting the first st on your right needle over the sl st and onto the left needle. Drop the needle that's in your right hand, and with the needle in your left hand, work the first half of your sts, letting the other needle hang. Work the second half of your sts using the other circ needle. Continue alternating needles as you work.

Whale Spine Cable Stitch (over 12 sts)

Rnds 1 and 2 K12.

Rnd 3 C6B (sl 3 sts to cn and hold to back, k3, k3 from cn), C6F (sl 3 sts to cn and hold to front, k3, k3 from cn).

Rnds 4–8 K12.

Rep rnds 1–12 for patt.

Directions

LEFT HAND

Using a stretchy CO method and smaller needles, CO 40 sts. Divide sts evenly over 2 needles. Pm and join.

Cuff

Work in k2, p2 rib for 2½".

Body

Change to larger needles.

Rnd 1 (inc) Needle 1 (palm), *p2, pfb, p2; rep from * to end. Needle 2 (back of hand), p2, pfb, p3, *k1, m1, k1; rep from * 3 times more, p3, pfb, p2—50 sts: 24 on Needle 1, 26 on Needle 2.

Rnd 2 Needle 1, purl. Needle 2, p7, work row 2 of Whale Spine Cable Stitch over next 12 sts, p7.

Cont in Rev St st and cable as est until glove meas 5" from beg.

Palm Chart

Next rnd Needle 1, p4, work row 1 of chart over next 11 sts, p9. Needle 2, cont in patt as est.

Cont in chart and patt as est until glove meas 5¼" from beg.

Thumb Opening

Next rnd Work to last 7 sts of Needle 1, with wy p7, slip these 7 sts back to LH needle and p7 with working yarn; work to end of rnd.

Cont working in patt as est until piece meas 7½" from beg. Place all sts on holders.

Thumb

Carefully remove wy from thumb opening, placing lower 7 sts onto Needle 1 and upper 8 sts onto Needle 2. Pm, PU 2 sts in gap between needles, p7, PU 2 sts in gap, p8—19 sts: 9 on Needle 1, 10 on Needle 2.

Next rnd Needle 1, p6, p2tog, p1. Needle 2, p7, p2tog, p1—17 sts.

Cont even in Rev St st for 1".

Next rnd Needle 1, [k1, p1] 4 times. Needle 2, [k1, p1] 3 times, k1, p2tog—16 sts.

Next rnd *K1, p1; rep from * around.

Using invisible BO method, BO.

Index Finger

Sl 6 sts from index finger edge of palm sts onto Needle 1 and 6 sts from back of hand sts onto Needle 2. Pm and join yarn to beg of Needle 1.

Next rnd Needle 1, purl. Needle 2, p to end, CO 2 sts—14 sts: 6 on Needle 1, 8 on Needle 2. Pm and join.

Work even in Rev St st for ¾".

Work in k1, p1 rib for 2 rnds.

Using invisible BO method, BO.

Pinky Finger

Sl 5 sts from pinky finger edge of palm sts onto Needle 1 and 5 sts from back of hand sts onto Needle 2. Pm and join yarn to beg of Needle 1.

Next rnd Needle 1, purl to end, CO 2 sts. Needle 2, purl—12 sts: 7 on Needle 1, 5 on Needle 2. Pm and join.

Work even in Rev St st for ⅝".

Work in k1, p1 rib for 2 rnds.

Using invisible BO method, BO.

Middle Finger

Sl 7 sts from index finger edge of palm sts to Needle 1 and 8 sts from back of hand sts to Needle 2. Pm and join yarn to beg of Needle 1.

Next rnd Needle 1, k to end, PU and k3 sts at base of index finger. Needle 2, k to end, CO 3 sts—21 sts: 10 on Needle 1, 11 on Needle 2.

Next rnd Needle 1, k6, k2tog twice. Needle 2, k3, k2tog, k6—18 sts: 8 on Needle 1, 10 on Needle 2.

Work even in St st for 1⅛".

Work in k1, p1 rib for 2 rnds.

Using invisible BO method, BO.

Ring Finger

Sl 6 sts from palm sts to Needle 1 and 7 sts from the back of hand sts to Needle 2. Pm and join yarn to beg of Needle 1.

Next rnd Needle 1, k to end, PU and k4 sts at base of middle finger. Needle 2, k to end, PU and k3 sts at base of pinky finger—20 sts: 10 on each needle.

Next rnd Needle 1, k5, k2tog, k3. Needle 2, k6, k2tog, k2—18 sts: 9 on each needle.

Work even in St st for 1".

Work in k1, p1 rib for 2 rnds.

BO *very loosely* in patt.

RIGHT HAND

Work same as for left hand until glove meas 5" from beg.

Palm Chart

1st rnd Needle 1, p9, work row 1 of chart over next

Palm Chart

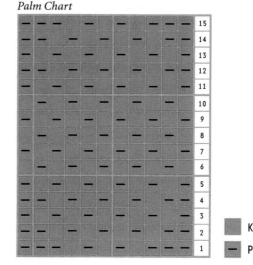

11 sts, p4. Needle 2, cont in patt as est.

Cont in chart and patt as est until glove meas 5¼" from beg.

Thumb Opening

1st rnd With wy, p7, slip these 7 sts back to LH needle and p7 with working yarn; work to end of rnd.

Work rem of glove same as for left hand, reversing shaping and finger placement as needed.

Weave in all ends.

About Kurt I came to knitting from a background in architecture—it was another outlet for my insatiable urge to create. As soon as I knitted my second row of stitches, I turned to my friend who was teaching me and said, "Oh! I'm making a grid!" and caught the fever immediately. I managed Knit n' Knibble, the most adorable knitting café, in Tampa, FL, for just under a year, and currently work as a salesman and teacher at the yarn mecca, Imagiknit (www.imagiknit.com), in San Francisco. While continuing to pursue architecture, I am launching a knitting design/made-to-measure knitted goods business as well as contributing to textile art shows.

Sizes

Finished width: 7"

Finished length: 60"

Materials

Alchemy *Synchronicity* (50% silk, 50% wool; 50g/118 yd), 4 skeins #30W Spruce

US 7 (4.5mm) straight needles

6 stitch markers

Safety pin

Cable needle

Gauge

26 sts and 22 rows = 4" in pattern

TISH DAVIDSON

Swelligant Scarf

After knitting scarves for all my female friends and family, I wanted to make an elegant scarf to give to the men and boys in my life. Cables were what I was after, but I wanted the scarf to look good on both sides. That's when I hit upon the wonderfully reversible cable stitch, used here, which yields a soft and drapeable scarf with little bulk that can be worn with business attire as easily as with a leather jacket. Worn folded in half lengthwise, wrapped around the neck with the ends pulled through will give it a really sporty look. The silk blend yarn I used adds luxury while looking classic and manly. After all, while he might not readily admit it, what man wouldn't enjoy the feel of silk next to his skin?

Special abbreviation

C8B: Sl 4 sts to cn and hold in back, [k1, p1] twice, then [k1, p1] twice from cn.

Directions

CO 40 sts loosely.

Row 1 K5, pm, *[k1, p1] 4 times, pm, k1, p1, k1, pm; rep from * once more, [k1, p1] 4 times, pm, k5.

Place safety pin at beg of row 1 to indicate RS of scarf, moving marker up as work progresses. Slip all markers as you come to them.

About Tish I knit extensively in college, then life overwhelmed my hobbies. Later I took up weaving and really enjoyed that fiber experience. Recently I injured my knee and could not climb the stairs to my loom or work the treadles. I started knitting again and can't stop. I love knitting's portability, the many exciting yarns and colors, the feel of it in my hands. I enjoy working up interesting patterns, and as a retired home economics teacher, I can't resist designing my own.

Rows 2–11 Sl 1, k4, *[k1, p1] 4 times, k1, p1, k1; rep from * once more, [k1, p1] 4 times, k5.

Row 12 Sl 1, k4, C8B, k1, p1, k1, [k1, p1] 4 times, k1, p1, k1, C8B, k5.

Rows 13–17 Rep row 2.

Row 18 Sl 1, k4, [k1, p1] 4 times, k1, p1, k1, C8B, k1, p1, k1, [k1, p1] 4 times, k5.

Rows 19–23 Rep row 2.

Row 24 Rep row 12.

Rep rows 13–24 to approx 1½" from desired finished length, ending with row 24.

Rep row 2 twelve times.

BO loosely.

Front

Back

Size

Finished width: 5½"

Finished length: 80"

Materials

Nashua Handknits *Creative Focus Worsted* (75% wool, 25% alpaca; 100g/220 yd)

Sushi Roll

A: 1 ball #1117 Grass

B: 1 ball #1636 Salmon

C: 3 balls #0100 Natural

D: 2 balls #3112 Evergreen

Happy Face

MC: 4 balls #1933 Goldenrod

CC: 1 ball #0500 Ebony

Size M/13 (9mm) crochet hook

1½ yards ½" elastic

Gauge

12 sts and 4 rows = 4" in double crochet holding 2 strands tog

NATASHA SILLS

Roll-Ups

This project is intended to be massively manly in every way; the exact opposite of the dainty, decorative girl-scarves that I usually make for myself. When worn, they appear to be simple scarves with haphazardly placed stripes, but when you roll them up, one becomes a giant sushi and the other a '70s smiley face. These magic roll-ups make an impressive presentation when gifting them to your guy—and he won't be able to resist demonstrating them to his friends afterward. The pattern is done in a simple double-crochet stitch, holding two strands of yarn together, so it works up quickly (quickly enough to exempt you from the standard pre-knit-ual agreement!). It may take a couple of tries to get the roll to look perfect, so don't get discouraged. If it looks funny the first time, try rerolling tighter or looser until the design works.

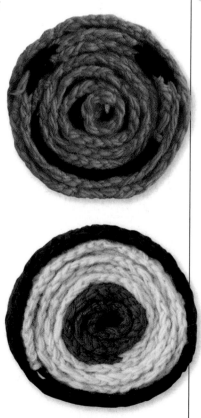

Directions

Note: Pattern is worked using 2 strands of yarn tog throughout.

Ch 18.

Row 1 Dc in 4th ch from hook and in each ch across—16 dc.

Row 2 Ch 3 (counts as first dc), dc in each dc across—16 dc.

Rep row 2 for patt.

For Sushi Roll, work above patt in foll color sequence:

6 rows A, 8 rows B, 41 rows C, 25 rows D.

For Happy Face, work above patt in foll color sequence:

17 rows MC, 1 row CC, 3 rows MC, 1 row CC, 8 rows MC, 1 row CC, 3 rows MC, 1 row CC, 2 rows MC, 6 rows CC, 37 rows MC.

FINISHING

Weave in ends. Tie elastic around rolled-up scarf to secure design in place.

About Natasha My obsession with needlework began when I bought a set of custom-knit pillow shams bearing the Transformers logo as a cheesy house-warming gift for my husband. When they arrived, they were incorrectly sized, full of holes, and unrecognizable as the logos I requested. I thought, "I bet I can do better than that." So I bought a copy of *Stitch 'n Bitch,* some needles, and two balls of Harry Potter's Gryffindor house colored yarn to practice on, and the rest is history. I have since learned to crochet and spin as well. I currently work at the Woolie Ewe yarn store in Plano, TX, and I chronicle my adventures and sell my wares online at www.GrittyKnits.com.

Size

S (M, L, XL, XXL)

Finished chest: 42 (46, 50, 54, 58)"

Finished length: 22 (24½, 24¾, 25, 27½)"

Materials

Knit Picks *Andean Silk* (55% alpaca, 23% silk, 22% wool; 50g/96 yd), 15 (16, 16, 17, 18) skeins #23520 cream

US 6 (4mm) 29" circular needle

US 8 (5mm) 29" circular needle or size needed to obtain gauge

US 6 (4mm) double-pointed needles (set of 5)

US 8 (5mm) double-pointed needles (set of 5)

Stitch markers

Cable needle

Waste yarn

Gauge

18½ sts and 26 rows = 4" in St st with larger needles

HEATHER DIXON

Cable Guy

I'm a big cable fan—I love the effects one can achieve by simply switching the order of stitches. Since no one ever told me that working cables was difficult, I attempted the technique without fear at a very early age, and have loved them ever since. For me, the wider I can make the cable, the more dramatic the effect. In this sweater I've used oversized, loosely twisted cables to create a manly and post-modern take on the traditional fisherman's sweater. Knit in the round and done up in a luxurious blend of cream-colored alpaca, silk, and super-soft merino wool, it looks classically rugged enough to suit the Ernest Hemingway in your life, yet is gentle enough for his sensitive side.

Special abbreviation

C12F: Sl 6 sts to cn and hold in front, k6, k6 from cn.

Directions

Note: To increase the sizes for this sweater, I added stitches to the purl sections of the pattern, meaning that the stitch will look slightly different when knit in the larger sizes.

BODY

With smaller circular needle, CO 260 (280, 300, 320, 340) sts. Pm and join.

Rnds 1–4 P0 (1, 1, 2, 2),*k12, p1 (2, 3, 4, 5); rep from * to last 0 (13, 14, 14, 15) sts, k0 (12, 12, 12, 12), p0 (1, 2, 2, 3).

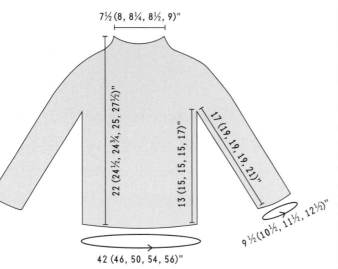

7½ (8, 8¼, 8½, 9)"

22 (24½, 24¾, 25, 27½)"

13 (15, 15, 15, 17)"

17 (19, 19, 19, 21)"

9½ (10½, 11½, 12½)"

42 (46, 50, 54, 56)"

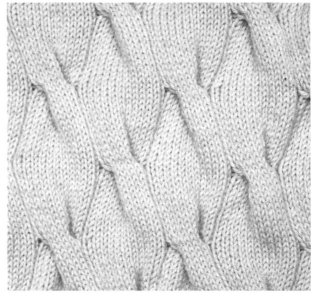

Change to larger needle and cont as foll:

Rnds 5–13 Rep rnd 1.

Rnd 14 (cable) P0 (1, 1, 2, 2), *C12F, p1 (2, 3, 4, 5), k12, p1 (2, 3, 4, 5); rep from * to last 0 (13, 14, 14, 15) sts, k0 (12, 12, 12, 12), p0 (1, 2, 2, 3).

Rnds 15–27 Rep rnd 1.

Rnd 28 (cable) P0 (1, 1, 2, 2), *k12, p1 (2, 3, 4, 5), C12F, p1 (2, 3, 4, 5); rep from * to last 0 (13, 14, 14, 15) sts, k0 (C12F, C12F, C12F, C12F), p0 (1, 2, 2, 3).

Rnds 29–41 Rep rnd 1.

Rep rnds 14–41 twice more—97 rnds.

Sizes M, L and XL only: Work rnds 14–27 once more—111 rnds.

Size XXL only: Work rnds 14–41 once more—125 rnds.

Place sts on wy.

SLEEVES (MAKE 2)

With smaller circular needle or dpns, CO 60 (64, 68, 72, 76) sts. Pm and join.

Rnds 1–3 K3 (3, 2, 2, 1), p1 (2, 3, 4, 5), *k12, p1 (2, 3, 4, 5); rep from * to last 4 (3, 3, 2, 2) sts, k4 (3, 3, 2, 2).

Change to larger circular needle or dpns and cont as foll:

Rnd 4 (cable) K3 (3, 2, 2, 1), p1 (2, 3, 3, 3), *C12F, p1 (2, 3, 4, 5), k12, p1 (2, 3, 4, 5); rep from * to last 4 (3, 3, 2, 2) sts, k4 (3, 3, 2, 2).

Rnds 5–8 Rep rnd 1.

Rnd 9 (inc) K1, m1, k2 (2, 1, 1, 0), p1 (2, 3, 3, 3), *k12, p1 (2, 3, 4, 5); rep from * to last 4 (3, 3, 2, 2) sts, k3 (2, 2, 1, 1), m1, k1—62 (66, 70, 74, 78) sts.

Rnds 10–17 K4 (4, 3, 3, 2), p1 (2, 3, 4, 4), *k12, p1 (2, 3, 4, 5); rep from * to last 5 (4, 4, 3, 3) sts, k5 (4, 4, 3, 3).

Rnd 18 (inc & cable) K1, m1, k3 (3, 2, 2, 1), p1 (2, 3, 4, 4), *k12, p1 (2, 3, 4, 5), C12F, p1 (2, 3, 4, 5); rep from * to last 5 (4, 4, 3, 3) sts, k4 (3, 3, 2, 2), m1, k1—64 (68, 72, 76, 80) sts.

Rnds 19–26 K5 (5, 4, 4, 3), p1 (2, 3, 4, 5), *k12, p1 (2, 3, 4, 5); rep from * to last 6 (5, 5, 4, 4) sts, k6 (5, 5, 4, 4).

Rnd 27 (inc) K1, m1, k4 (4, 3, 3, 2), p1 (2, 3, 4, 5), *k12, p1 (2, 3, 4, 5); rep from * to last 6 (5, 5, 4, 4) sts, k5 (4, 4, 3, 3), m1, k1—66 (70, 74, 78, 82) sts.

Rnds 28–31 K6 (6, 5, 5, 4), p1 (2, 3, 4, 5), *k12, p1 (1, 2, 3, 4, 5); rep from * to last 7 (6, 6, 5, 5) sts, k7 (6, 6, 5, 5).

Rnd 32 (cable) K6 (6, 5, 5, 4), p1 (2, 3, 4, 5), *C12F, p1 (2, 3, 4, 5), k12, p1 (2, 3, 4, 5); rep from * to last 7 (6, 6, 5, 5) sts, k7 (6, 6, 5, 5).

Rnds 33–35 K6 (6, 5, 5, 4), p1 (2, 3, 4, 5), *k12, p1 (2, 3, 4, 5); rep from * to last 7 (6, 6, 5, 5) sts, k7 (6, 6, 5, 5).

Rnd 36 (inc) K1, m1, k5 (5, 4, 4, 3), p1 (2, 3, 4, 5), *k12, p1 (2, 3, 4, 5); rep from * to last 7 (6, 6, 5, 5) sts, k6 (5, 5, 4, 4, m1, k1—68 (72, 76, 80, 84) sts.

Rnds 37–44 K7 (7, 6, 6, 5), p1 (2, 3, 4, 5), *k12, p1 (2, 3, 4, 5); rep from * to last 8 (7, 7, 6, 6) sts, k8 (7, 7, 6, 6).

Rnd 45 (inc) K1, m1, k6 (6, 5, 5, 4), p1 (2, 3, 4, 5), *k12, p1 (2, 3, 4, 5); rep from * to last 8 (7, 7, 6, 6) sts, k7 (6, 6, 5, 5), m1, k1—70 (74, 78, 82, 86) sts.

Rnd 46 (cable) K8 (8, 7, 7, 6), p1 (2, 3, 4, 5), * k12, p1 (2, 3, 4, 5), C12F, p1 (2, 3, 4, 5); rep from * to last 9 (8, 8, 7, 7) sts, k9 (8, 8, 7, 7).

Rnds 47–53 K8 (8, 7, 7, 6), p1 (2, 3, 4, 5), *k12, p1 (2, 3, 4, 5); rep from * to last 9 (8, 8, 7, 7) sts, k9 (8, 8, 7, 7).

Rnd 54 (inc) K1, m1, k7 (7, 6, 6, 5), p1 (2, 3, 4, 5), *k12, p1 (2, 3, 4, 5); rep from * to last 9 (8, 8, 7, 7) sts, k8 (7, 7, 6, 6), m1, k1—72 (76, 80, 84, 88) sts.

Rnds 55–59 K9 (9, 8, 8, 7), p1 (2, 3, 4, 5), *k12, p1 (2, 3, 4, 5); rep from * to last 10 (9, 9, 8, 8) sts, k10 (9, 9, 8, 8).

Rnd 60 (cable) K9 (9, 8, 8, 7), p1 (2, 3, 4, 5), *C12F, p1 (2, 3, 4, 5), k12, p1 (2, 3, 4, 5); rep from * to last 10 (9, 9, 8, 8) sts, k10 (9, 9, 8, 8).

Rnds 61–62 K9 (9, 8, 8, 7), p1 (2, 3, 4, 5), *k12, p1 (2, 3, 4, 5); rep from * to last 10 (9, 9, 8, 8) sts, k10 (9, 9, 8, 8).

Rnd 63 (inc) K1, m1, k8 (8, 7, 7, 6), p1 (2, 3, 4, 5); *k12, p1 (2, 3, 4, 5); rep from * to last 10 (9, 9, 8, 8) sts, k9 (8, 8, 7, 7), m1, k1—74 (78, 82, 86, 90) sts.

Rnds 64–71 K10 (10, 9, 9, 8), p1 (2, 3, 4, 5); *k12, p1 (2, 3, 4, 5); rep from * to last 11 (10, 10, 9, 9) sts, k11 (10, 10, 9, 9).

Rnd 72 (inc) K1, m1, k9 (9, 8, 8, 7), p1 (2, 3, 4, 5); *k12, p1 (2, 3, 4, 5); rep from * to last 11 (10, 10, 9, 9) sts, k10 (9, 9, 8, 8), m1, k1—76 (80, 84, 88, 92) sts.

Rnd 73 K11 (11, 10, 10, 9), p1 (2, 3, 4, 5); *k12, p1 (2, 3, 4, 5); rep from * to last 12 (11, 11, 10, 10) sts, k12 (11, 11, 10, 10).

Rnd 74 (cable) K11 (11, 10, 10, 9), p1 (2, 3, 4, 5), * k12, p1 (2, 3, 4, 5), C12F, p1 (2, 3, 4, 5); rep from * to last 12 (11, 11, 10, 10) sts, k12 (11, 11, 10, 10).

Rnds 75–87 K11 (11, 10, 10, 9), p1 (2, 3, 4, 5); *k12, p1 (2, 3, 4, 5); rep from * to last 12 (11, 11, 10, 10) sts, k12 (11, 11, 10, 10).

Rnd 88 (cable) K11 (11, 10, 10, 9), p1 (2, 3, 4, 5); *C12F, p1 (2, 3, 4, 5), k12, p1 (2, 3, 4, 5); rep from * to last 12 (11, 11, 10, 10) sts, k12.

Rnds 89–101 Rep rnd 75.

Rnds 102–129 Rep rnds 74–101.

Sizes M, L and XL only: Rep rnds 74–87.

Size XXL only: Rep rnds 74–101.

K6 and place last 12 sts onto wy. Place sts onto holder. Work second sleeve, keeping sts on the needle.

JOIN BODY TO SLEEVES

Place first 6 and last 6 sts of body onto wy.

Rnd 1 (join) *Left sleeve:* K5 (5, 4, 4, 3), p1 (2, 3, 4, 5), patt to last 6 sts, k6 (5, 5, 4, 4), pm; *Front:* K6 (7, 7, 8, 8), p1 (2, 3, 4, 5), cont in patt across Front sts to 13 (13, 14, 14, 15) sts before marker, k7 (7, 8, 8, 9), pm; place next 12 sts onto wy; for *Right sleeve and Back:* rep from *, end at pm—364 (392, 420, 448, 476) sts. Last marker indicates beg of rnd at back left shoulder.

Rnd 2 (dec) *K2, k2tog, work in patt as est to 4 sts from next marker, ssk, k2; rep from * 3 times more—8 sts dec; 356 (384, 412, 440, 468) sts.

Rnd 3 Work even in patt as est, always keeping the 2 sts before and after each marker in St st.

Keeping in patt as est, rep rnds 2 and 3 until 188 (216, 236, 264, 276) sts rem—22 (22, 23, 23, 25) times total. Then rep rnd 2 twice, rnd 3 once, and rnd 2 5 (7, 8, 10, 10) times more—132 (144, 156, 168, 180) sts.

NECK SHAPING

Rnd 1 *K2, k2tog, work in patt as est to 5 sts from next marker, ssk, k2, sm, k1, k2tog, ssk, k1, sm; rep from * once more—124 (136, 148, 160, 172) sts.

Rnd 2 *K2, k2tog, work in patt as est to 4 sts from next marker, ssk, k2, sm, k2tog, ssk, sm; rep from * once more—116 (128, 140, 152, 164) sts.

Rnd 3 *K2, k2tog, work in patt as est to 4 sts from next marker, ssk, k2, sm, ssk, sm; rep from * once more—110 (122, 134, 146, 160) sts.

Rnd 4 *K2, k2tog, work in patt as est to 4 sts from next marker, ssk, k2, sm, k1, sm; rep from * once more—106 (118, 130, 142, 154) sts.

Rep last rnd 3 (5, 7, 9, 11) times more—94 (98, 102, 106, 110) sts.

Change to smaller needles.

K 9 rows.

FINISHING

Bind off loosely. Graft underarm sts. Weave in ends. Block to shape if necessary.

About Heather I have a serious yarn addiction. With stashes at my home, office, boyfriend's apartment, friend's attic, and parents' house, I'm never far from spontaneously starting a new project. After studying knitwear design in my native England, I moved to New York City, which has been my home for the past ten years. I spend my time designing, writing patterns, teaching knitting, and playing with yarn. My patterns have been published in various media, and last year I published my own book: *Not Your Mamma's Knitting*. Follow my adventures on my blog, armyofknitters.blogspot.com.

LAURA BENNETT

Cobra

This simple and contemporary sweater design was born of a collaborative process involving several men who are pretty persnickety when it comes to what they wear. The shape of the sweater is inspired by the ever-popular fleece sweatshirts. The stripes are inspired by my dad's AC Shelby Cobra (a famous roadster from the 1960s), and I suppose there's something snakelike about the zipper at the neck as well, as it can open to allow even the largest of heads to slip comfortably through. I made it using a moderately priced alpaca blend that men seem particularly drawn to because it is lightweight, warm, and has an understated softness. The contemporary simplicity of this design is made easy because I wrote the pattern so that you can knit almost all of the body and the sleeves in the round. Life is so much happier when there are fewer ends to work away!

Size

S (M, L, XL)

Finished chest: 42 (44, 48, 52)"

Finished length: 24 (25, 26, 27)"

Materials

Berroco *Ultra Alpaca* (50% alpaca, 50% wool; 100g/215 yd)

MC: 4 (4, 5, 6) hanks #6289 Charcoal Mix

CC: 1 hank #6281 Redwood Mix

US 8 (5mm) 16" and 36" circular needles, or size needed to obtain gauge

US 8 (5mm) double-pointed needles (set of 5)

Waste yarn

7"–9" invisible zipper in black

Sewing needle and matching thread

Gauge

20 sts and 24 rows = 4" in St st

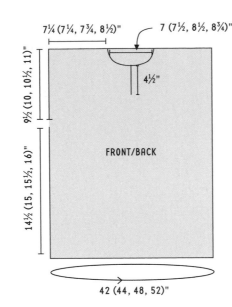

7¼ (7¼, 7¾, 8½)"

7 (7½, 8½, 8¾)"

9½ (10, 10½, 11)"

4½"

FRONT/BACK

14½ (15, 15½, 16)"

42 (44, 48, 52)"

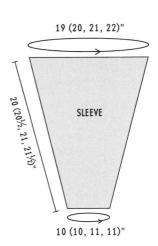

19 (20, 21, 22)"

20 (20½, 21, 21½)"

SLEEVE

10 (10, 11, 11)"

Directions
BODY
With longer circular needle and MC, CO 212 (220, 240, 260) sts. Pm and join. Work in k2, p2 rib for 6 rnds. Change to CC and cont in rib for 4 rnds. Change to MC and cont in rib for 2 rnds, then work in St st until body meas 14½ (15, 15½, 16)" from beg. Place last 106 (110, 120, 130) sts on wy for front.

BACK
Working back and forth on next 106 (110, 120, 130) sts, cont even in St st for 8½ (9, 9½, 10)", ending with a WS row.

Neck shaping
Next row (RS) K45 (45, 48, 52), join 2nd ball of MC and BO center 16 (20, 24, 26) sts, k to end.

Working both sides at the same time, BO 3 sts at neck edge 3 times—36 (36, 39, 43) sts each side. BO.

FRONT
Place front sts onto needle and work even in St st for 3½ (4, 4½, 5)", ending with a WS row.

Neck shaping
Left side
Row 1 (RS) K49 (51, 56, 61), [p1, k1] twice, place rem 53 (55, 60, 65) sts on wy for right side.

Row 2 [K1, p1] twice, p to end.

Rep rows 1 and 2 for 4½", ending with a RS row.

BO 8 (10, 10, 10) sts at neck edge.

Sizes S and M only: At neck edge, BO 3 sts once, then 2 sts 3 times—36 (36) sts.

Size L only: At neck edge, BO 3 sts 3 times, then 2 sts once—39 sts.

Size XL only: At neck edge, BO 3 sts 4 times—43 sts.

BO all sts.

Right side

Place sts of right side onto needle and join yarn to beg with a RS row.

Row 1 (RS) [K1, p1] twice, k to end.

Row 2 P49 (51, 56, 61), [p1, k1] twice.

Rep rows 1 and 2 for 4½", ending with a WS row.

Complete right side as for left side, reversing shaping.

SLEEVES (MAKE 2)

With dpns and MC, CO 52 (52, 56, 56) sts. Divide evenly over 4 needles, pm and join. Work in k2, p2 rib for 12 rnds. Work in St st, changing to circular needle when possible.

Inc rnd M1, k to last st, m1, k1.

Cont in St st, rep inc rnd every 4th rnd 10 (18, 17, 22) times more, then every 6th rnd 10 (5, 6, 4) times—94 (100, 104, 110) sts. AT THE SAME TIME, when sleeve meas 14½ (15, 15½, 16)" from beg, cont incs as est, change to CC and work 4 rnds St st, change to MC and work 7 rnds St st, change to CC and work 4 rnds St st, then change to MC and complete incs. Work even in St st until sleeve meas 20 (20½, 21, 21½)" from beg. BO.

FINISHING

Sew shoulder seams. Sew sleeves into armholes.

Collar

With RS facing, short circular needle and MC, PU and k78 (86, 94, 98) sts evenly around neck opening. Work in k2, p2 rib, beg with p2 on first row, for 4 rows. Change to CC and cont in rib for 4 rows. Change to MC and cont in rib for 4 rows. BO in rib.

Zipper Placement

Using wy, loosely baste together edges where zipper is to be placed. Place zipper on the inside of sweater with zipper pull against basted edges. With sewing needle and thread, baste zipper in place. Using a sewing machine or by hand, sew zipper in place. Remove all basting sts and test zipper.

Weave in ends.

About Laura By day I am an environmental geologist. At night and on weekends I can be found knitting, quilting, print-making, and painting. Knitting is my favorite indulgence in color, texture, and clothing. I can't remember when I learned to knit, but I'm sure it was my mom who taught me how. I put it aside for several years when I spent most of my after-school hours in my grandma's scrap fabric bag, designing all kinds of creations for my Barbie and troll dolls and for myself. I am very fortunate that my mom and grandma saved me from a lot of extra preteen embrassment by making most of the things I designed for myself disappear. I live and work in Salt Lake City, UT, with my husband, Mike, and our two adopted furballs. You can keep up on my exploits with yarn at lulupurl.blogspot.com.

KAREN BAUMER

Mr. Stripey

Mr. Stripey came about when I wanted to make a colorful sweater that would be more interesting than plain stockinette stripes, and that would let the shades interact with each other without creating too much extra bulk. I opted for a slip-stitch color pattern because it is an easy way to get complicated-looking color work without having to manipulate multiple strands of yarn at once. This version is done in a funky, retro-hipster color scheme, but could just as easily be made in something more subtle, such as various shades of natural browns and tan, or perhaps in a nautical look with shades of navy and white (the ribbing sections would look great with just the cast-on row done in red).

Size

S (M, L, XL, XXL)

Finished chest: 44 (47, 50, 53, 56)"

Finished length: 27 (27, 28, 28, 28½)"

Materials

Cascade Yarns *ECO+*
(100% wool; 250g/478 yd)

MC: 2 hanks #0958 Cinnamon

CC1: 1 (1, 1, 2, 2) hank(s) #7009 Kiwi

CC2: 1 (1, 1, 2, 2) hank(s) #2749 Pumpkin

US 10 (6mm) straight needles, or size needed to obtain gauge

US 8 (5mm) 16" circular needle

Gauge

18 sts and 32 rows = 4" in Garter Slip st on larger needles

Garter Slip Stitch

Row 1 (RS) Knit.

Row 2 Knit.

Row 3 K1, *sl 1 wyib, k1; rep from * across.

Row 4 K1, *sl 1 wyif, k1; rep from * across.

Rep rows 1–4 for patt.

Color sequence

Rows 1 and 2 Work in MC.

Rows 3 and 4 Work in CC1.

Rows 5 and 6 Work in CC2.

Rep rows 1–6 in Garter Slip Stitch patt.

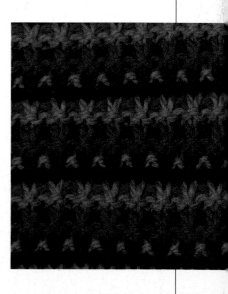

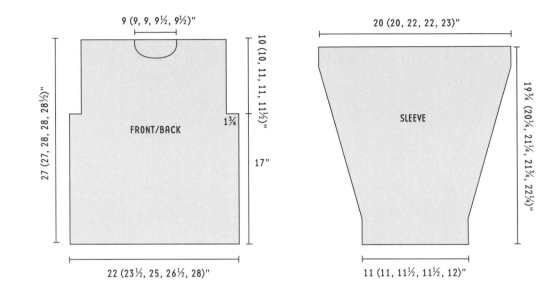

9 (9, 9, 9½, 9½)"

10 (10, 11, 11, 11½)"

FRONT/BACK

1¾

17"

27 (27, 28, 28, 28½)"

22 (23½, 25, 26½, 28)"

20 (20, 22, 22, 23)"

SLEEVE

19¾ (20¼, 21¼, 21¾, 22¼)"

11 (11, 11½, 11½, 12)"

Directions

BACK

With smaller needles and MC, CO 98 (106, 112, 120, 126) sts and work in k2, p2 rib for 2½", inc 1 st on last WS row—99 (107, 113, 121, 127) sts. Change to larger needles and beg working Garter Slip Stitch patt foll color sequence. When work meas 17" from beg, BO 8 sts at beg of next 2 rows—83 (91, 97, 105, 111) sts. Cont in patt as est, work even until armhole meas 10 (10, 11, 11, 11½)", ending with a WS row. BO.

FRONT

Work as for back until work is 3" (24 rows) shorter than back, ending with a WS row.

Next row Work 31 (35, 38, 41, 44) sts, BO 21 (21, 21, 23, 23) sts, work to end. Complete each side of neck separately, keeping in patt as est, as foll: Dec 1 st at neck edge every other row 5 times—26 (30, 33, 36, 39) sts, then work even until meas matches back. Work other side of neck to match.

SLEEVES (MAKE 2)

With smaller needle and MC, CO 50 (50, 52, 52, 54) sts and work in k2, p2 rib for 2½", inc 1 st on last WS row—51 (51, 53, 53, 55) sts. Change to larger needles and begin working Garter Slip Stitch patt foll color sequence, and AT THE SAME TIME beg sleeve shaping as foll: Keeping in patt as est and working additional sts into patt, inc 1 st each side on the 7th row, then every foll 8th row 8 (8, 9, 9, 10) times and then every foll 4th row 11 (11, 13, 13, 13) times—91 (91, 99, 99, 103) sts. Work even until sleeve meas 19¾ (20¼, 21¼, 21¾, 22¼)" from beg, ending with a WS row. BO.

FINISHING

Sew shoulder seams.

Neckband

With RS facing, circular needle and MC, starting at left shoulder seam, PU 88 (88, 88, 92, 92) sts around neck opening as foll: 17 sts down left side front, 21 (21, 21, 23, 23) sts across front, 17 sts up right side front, and 33 (33, 33, 35, 35) sts across back neck. Pm and join. Work in k2, p2 rib for 3". BO loosely, leaving a long tail for sewing. Fold ribbing in half to inside and sew down BO edge neatly and evenly around.

Sew sleeves into armhole openings. Sew side and sleeve seams. Weave in ends.

About Karen I grew up in San Diego and learned knitting from my mom when I was fourteen. Two years later I finished high school and moved to Germany, where at the time (mid-1980s) knitting was much more common and good yarn far more readily available than in the U.S. I moved back to the States at age eighteen, and since then I've earned two postgraduate degrees (in linguistics and Germanic languages and literatures) and now work as a linguist at a San Francisco legal services/consulting firm. That job keeps me very busy, but I manage to submit a couple of patterns every year for publication, and I've appeared several times as a guest instructor on the DIY channel's *Knitty Gritty* show. My preferred knitting background music is Bob Dylan or any of Mozart's operas.

JENNIFER HAGAN

Pub Crawler

This is the perfect sweater for a stout night out. Its beautiful cable stitch work and Celtic tattooed armband detail will have your man's Irish eyes smiling, even if he's Italian. He won't wear it just because you made it, but because of its unique, sexy style. If you don't think he'd like the brown and blue shown here, consider gray and blue, maroon and green, or even two shades of the same hue for subtlety. It's guaranteed to be a favorite for you to knit and for him to wear.

Special abbreviations

C4B: Sl 2 sts to cn and hold in back, k2, k2 from cn.

T3B: Sl 1 st to cn and hold in back, k2, p1 from cn.

T3F: Sl 2 sts to cn and hold in front, p1, k2 from cn.

Long Cable Rib pattern
(multiple of 12 sts plus 6)

Rows 1, 3 and 5 (RS) P2, *k2, p2; rep from * to end.

Row 2 (and all even rows) K the knit sts and p the purl sts.

Row 7 P2, *k2, p2, T3F, T3B, p2, rep to last 4 sts, k2, p2.

Row 9 P2, *k2, p3, C4B, p3; rep to last 4 sts, k2, p2.

Row 11 P2, *k2, p2, T3B, T3F, p2; rep to last 4 sts, k2, p2.

Row 12 Rep row 2.

Rep rows 1–12 for patt.

Size
S (M, L, XL, XXL)

Finished chest: 39 (43, 47, 51, 55)"

Finished length: 25 (26½, 27½, 29½, 31)"

Materials
Cascade Yarns *Cascade 220* (100% wool; 100g/220 yd)

MC: 3 (4, 4, 5, 5) hanks #9452 multicolor blue

CC: 2 (2, 3, 3, 3) hanks #8013 tan

US 7 (4.5mm) 16" and 24" circular needles or sizes needed to obtain gauge

US 6 (4mm) 16" circular needle

Cable needle

Gauge
20 sts and 24 rows = 4" in St st on larger needles

Directions

BACK

With 24" needle and MC, CO 98 (108, 118, 128, 138) sts.

Set-up row

For size S only: P2, k2, work in cable patt over next 90 sts, k2, p2.

For size M only: P1, k2, work in cable patt over next 102 sts, k2, p1.

For size L only: K2, work in cable patt over next 114 sts, k2.

For size XL only: P1, k2, p2, k2, work in cable patt over next 114 sts, k2, p2, k2, p1.

For size XXL only: Work in cable patt over 138 sts.

Work in rib and cable patt as est until back meas 15½ (16, 16, 17, 17½)" or desired length, ending with a WS row.

Armhole Shaping

BO 5 (6, 7, 7, 7) sts at beg of next 2 rows.

Dec row Ssk, work in patt to last 2 sts, k2tog.

Rep dec row every RS row 3 (4, 6, 6, 6) times more—80 (86, 90, 100, 110) sts. Cont even in patt as est until armholes meas 8½ (9½, 10½, 11½, 12½)", ending with a WS row.

Shoulder and Neck Shaping

BO 7 (8, 8, 9, 10) sts at beg of next row.

BO 7 (8, 8, 9, 10) sts at beg of next row, work 14 (15, 15, 17, 19) sts, BO center 36 (40, 44, 48, 52) sts, work across rem sts.

Right shoulder

BO 7 (7, 7, 8, 9) sts, work to end of row, turn. P2tog, work to end of row. BO rem sts.

Left shoulder

With WS facing, join yarn to sts of left shoulder.

BO 7 (7, 7, 8, 9) sts, work to end of row, turn. K2tog, work to end of row. BO rem sts.

FRONT

Work same as Back until armholes meas 6½ (7½, 8½, 9½, 10½)", ending with a WS row.

Neck and Shoulder Shaping

Work 28 (30, 29, 34, 38) sts, BO center 24 (26, 32, 32, 34) sts, work across rem sts.

Right shoulder

Next row (WS) Work even in patt as est.

Next row (dec) Ssk, work in patt to end of row—27 (29, 28, 33, 37) sts.

Rep last 2 rows 6 (7, 6, 8, 9) times more.

AT THE SAME TIME, when piece meas 23 (25, 26, 28½, 30)", BO 8 (8, 8, 9, 10) sts at armhole edge once, then BO 7 (7, 7, 8, 9) sts at armhole edge twice.

Left shoulder

With WS facing, join yarn to sts of left shoulder.

Next row (WS) Work even in patt as est.

Next row (dec) Work to last 2 sts, k2tog.

Work rem of left shoulder same as right shoulder.

RIGHT SLEEVE

With larger 16" needle and CC, CO 50 (50, 54, 54, 58) sts. Work in k2, p2 rib, beg with p2.

Inc 1 st each side of every 4th row 0 (12, 10, 13, 15) times; every 6th row 10 (7, 9, 8, 7) times; then every 8th row 3 (0, 0, 0, 0) times, working all new sts into patt—76 (88, 92, 96, 102) sts.

Tattoo Band

Change to smaller needles and work 12 rows of Tattoo Chart, ending on RS with st 6 (4, 1, 5, 4) and beg on WS

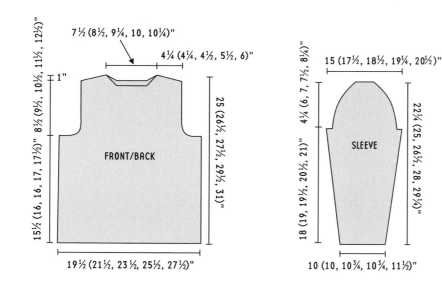

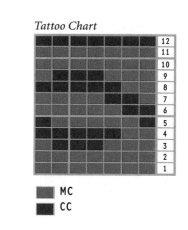

Tattoo Chart

■ MC
■ CC

with st 6 (4, 1, 5, 4). Break off MC.

Change to larger needles and work even in rib patt until sleeve measures 18 (19, 19½, 20½, 21)" from beg.

Shape Sleeve Cap

BO 6 (6, 7, 7, 7) sts at beg of next 2 rows—64 (76, 78, 82, 88) sts. Dec 1 st each side of every RS row 5 (9, 18, 17, 21) times, then every row 9 (12, 0, 6, 2) times—36 (34, 42, 36, 42) sts. BO 3 (2, 3, 2, 3) sts at beg of next 2 rows, and 3 (3, 4, 2, 3) sts at beg of foll 2 rows. BO rem 24 (24, 28, 28, 30) sts.

LEFT SLEEVE

Work same as right sleeve, substituting 12 rows even in rib for tattoo band.

FINISHING
Neckband

Sew shoulder seams.

With RS facing, smaller needle and CC, starting at left shoulder seam, PU and k10 (12, 12, 10, 10) sts down left front neck, 24 (26, 32, 32, 34) sts across center front neck, 10 (12, 12, 10, 10) sts up right front neck, 2 (3, 2, 2, 3) sts down right back neck, 36 (40, 44, 48, 52) sts across center back neck, and 2 (3, 2, 2, 3) sts up left back neck—84 (96, 104, 104, 112) sts. Pm and join.

Work 12 rows k2, p2 rib as foll:

For sizes S and XL only: K1, p2, *k2, p2; rep from *, end k1.

For sizes M and XXL only: *K2, p2; rep from * to end.

For size L only: P1, *k2, p2; rep from *, end k2, p1.

BO in rib.

Set in sleeves, sew side and sleeve seams. Weave in ends. Block lightly.

About Jennifer My first needlework love was crochet. Then I fell for embroidery. I took up knitting when I was in college, and I haven't stopped since. I clicked the needles a bunch when my three daughters were little, but singing in a band and then a stint teaching high school English caused a major slowdown for a few years. That's when I fixed it so that I could knit all the time, and started my own design business. Visit my design site, www.figheadh.com, and my blog, figknits.blogspot.com, to see what I've been up to lately.

Size

S (M, L, XL, XXL)

Finished chest: 43 (47½, 52, 56½, 61)"

Finished length: 26 (26½, 27½, 28½, 29)"

Materials

Cleckheaton *Country 8-ply* (100% wool; 50g/106 yd)

MC: 12 (12, 13, 13, 14) skeins #0003 white

CC1: 1 skein #0048 navy

CC2: 1 skein #0018 burgundy

US 7 (4.5mm) straight needles, or size needed to obtain gauge

US 5 (3.75mm) straight and 16" circular needles

Cable needle

Stitch holders or waste yarn

Stitch marker

Gauge

28 sts and 25½ rows = 4" in cable and rib patt using larger needles

KATE CHIOCCHIO

Love

This started off as a sweater my father asked my grandmother to make for him in the eighties—long before I became a knitter. He wanted a classic Davis Cup–type tennis sweater with cables and snug ribbing at the waist. Her first attempt ended just above his belly button and the sleeves went past his fingertips. After her second attempt came out exactly like the first, my father gave up. Twenty years later, I celebrated my own interest in tennis with a purple and eggplant-trimmed cabled hoodie. My father took one look at it and said, "You're a bit better than your grandmother was." This pattern reflects his requirements for the perfect tennis vest: a high V-neck, finished in two-by-two-ribbing, that's roomy enough to allow for ease of movement on the court. And while this classic piece could be worn on center court at Wimbledon or your own neighborhood tennis court, it would look equally smashing in muted blues, greens, and grays at the office or out on the town.

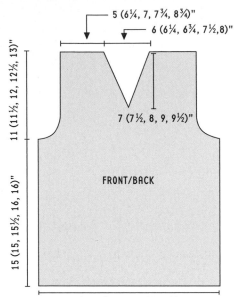

5 (6¼, 7, 7¾, 8¾)"

6 (6¼, 6¾, 7½, 8)"

11 (11½, 12, 12½, 13)"

7 (7½, 8, 9, 9½)"

15 (15, 15½, 16, 16)"

FRONT/BACK

21½ (23¾, 26, 28½, 30½)"

Special abbreviation

C6B: Sl 3 sts to cn and hold to back, k3, k3 from cn.

Directions

BACK

With smaller needles and CC1, cable CO 150 (166, 182, 198, 214) sts.

Row 1 (RS) K2, *p2, k2; rep from * to end.

Row 2 P2, *k2, p2; rep from * to end.

Rows 3 and 4 With CC2, rep rows 1 and 2.

Rows 5–12 With MC, rep rows 1 and 2.

Change to larger needles, and work in cable and rib patt as foll:

Rows 1 and 3 (RS) K6, *p2, k6; rep from * to end.

Rows 2 and 4 P6, *k2, p6; rep from * to end.

Sizes S, L and XXL only:

Row 5 K6, *p2, C6B, p2, k6; rep from * to end.

Sizes M and XL only:

Row 5 K6, p2, k6, *p2, C6B, p2, k6; rep from * to last 8 sts, p2, k6.

Row 6 Rep row 2.

Rep Rows 1–6 until piece meas 15 (15, 15½, 16, 16)" from beg, ending with a WS row.

Shape Armholes

BO 7 sts at beg of next 2 rows—136 (152, 168, 184, 200) sts.

Dec row (RS) K1, ssk, work in patt as est to last 3 sts, k2tog, k1.

Cont in patt as est, rep dec row every RS row 10 times more—114 (130, 146, 162, 178) sts. Cont even in patt as est until armhole meas 11 (11½, 12, 12½, 13)". Place first and last 36 (43, 49, 55, 61) sts on holders for right and left shoulders and center 42 (44, 48, 52, 56) sts on holder for back neck.

FRONT

Work same as back until armhole meas 4 (4, 4, 3½, 3½)", ending with row 3 of patt.

Shape Neck

Work 50 (58, 66, 74, 82) sts in patt, k2tog, p2, k3; join a 2nd skein of MC; k3, p2, ssk, work in patt as est to end—56 (64, 72, 80, 88) sts each side.

Work both sides at the same time as foll:

Row 1 (WS) Work even in patt as est.

Row 2 *For left front,* work in patt as est to last 7 sts, k2tog, p2, k3; *for right front,* k3, p2, ssk, work in patt as est to end.

Rep last 2 rows 19 (20, 22, 24, 26) times more—36 (43, 49, 55, 61) sts each shoulder. Work even in patt as est on both shoulders until armholes meas same as back. Keep sts on needle.

FINISHING

Join front and back shoulders using 3-needle BO. Sew side seams from armhole to bottom.

Neckband

With RS facing, circular needle and MC, starting at right shoulder seam, work as foll:

Size S only: P2, *k2, p2; rep from * to end of back neck sts.

Sizes M and XL only: K1, p2, *k2, p2; rep from * to last back neck st, k1.

Sizes L and XXL only: P1, *k2, p2; rep from * to last 3 back neck sts, k2, p1.

Cont around front neck, PU and k39 (42, 44, 49, 51) sts to base of V-neck, pm, PU and k39 (42, 44, 49, 51) sts to beg—120 (128, 136, 150, 158) sts. Pm and join. Change to CC2.

Rnd 1 Work in rib as est across back neck sts, and cont around as foll:

Size S only: P2, *k2, p2; rep from * to 5 sts from marker, k2, p1, k2tog, sm, ssk, p1, k2, **p2, k2; rep from ** to last 2 sts, p2.

Sizes M and XL only: K1, p2, *k2, p2; rep from * to 3 (2) sts from marker, k1 (0), k2tog, sm, ssk, k1 (0), **p2, k2; rep from ** to last 3 sts, p2, k1.

Sizes L and XXL only: P1, *k2, p2; rep from * to 3 (2) sts from marker, k1 (0), k2tog, sm, ssk, k1 (0), **p2, k2; rep from ** to last st, p1.

Rnd 2 Work in rib as est to 2 sts from next marker, k2tog, sm, ssk, cont in rib as est to end.

Change to CC1, and rep rnd 2 twice. BO in rib.

Armbands

With RS facing, using circular needle and MC, starting at underarm seam, PU and k108 (112, 116, 124, 128) sts evenly around armhole. Pm and join. Change to CC2 and work in k2, p2 rib for 2 rnds. Change to CC1 and cont in rib for 2 rnds. BO in rib.

Rep for other armhole.

Weave in ends. Block to measurements.

About Kate When my mom taught me to knit at age eight, I knit my grandfather a red scarf for Christmas and didn't knit again until many years later. After decades of resisting traditionally feminine activities, I became fascinated with fabric, particularly its color and texture, and, by extension, fiber. When I picked up my needles again, I quickly became obsessed and started a neighborhood Stitch 'n Bitch with some friends. Now I have a fledgling fiber business so I can spend all my time knitting, dyeing, and spinning. In the evenings, when I knit and watch tennis, I think about my grandmother who spent hers knitting and watching baseball.

ROBYN CHACHULA

Blueprint

When creating garments for the men in my life, there are two things that drive me. First, I want them to actually wear them, so I tend to make projects that are as functional as possible. A zip-up vest can be worn every day and it can take a lot of beatings. Second, I want them to like it, so I use my architectural flair to come up with cool geometric lines. With these goals in mind, I recently designed a crocheted vest for my seven-year-old nephew, and I knew I'd hit the jackpot when my husband, step-dad, and brother-in-law all requested one in their size. So the grown-up version was born. The simple horizontal stripes are spaced closer together as they travel up the vest and are bisected by vertical lines at the one-third point, reminding me of cool skyscraper windows. This pattern has the added bonus of drawing your attention to the face, which I also love. The vest is made large enough to fit over many layers, and is comfortable enough for daily wear. I hope all your men enjoy it as much as mine do.

Size

S (M, L, XL, XXL)

Finished chest: 35 (39, 43, 47, 51)"

Materials

Mission Falls *1824 Wool* (100% merino superwash wool; 50g/85 yd)

MC: 10 (11, 13, 16, 19) skeins #022 Ink

CC: 2 (2, 3, 3, 4) skeins #0533 Squash

Size J/10 (6mm) crochet hook

One 28 (28, 28, 30, 30)" coil separating zipper

Sewing needle and matching thread

Gauge

13 sts = 4" and 8 rows = 4½" alternating rows of LTR and sc through front lp only

Linked Treble Crochet (LTR)

Beg LTR: Insert hook in 2nd ch from hook, yo and pull up lp, skip 1 ch, insert hook in next ch, yo and pull up lp, insert hook in first st, yo and pull up lp (4 lps on hook), [yo and draw through 2 lps] 3 times.

LTR: Insert hook into upper horizontal bar of previous st, yo and pull up lp, insert hook into lower horizontal bar, yo and pull up lp, insert hook in next st, yo and pull up lp (4 lps on hook), [yo and draw through 2 lps] 3 times.

Linked Double Crochet (LDC)

Beg LDC: Insert hook in 2nd ch from hook, yo and pull up lp, skip 1 ch, insert hook in next st, yo and pull up lp (3 lps on hook), [yo and draw through 2 lps] twice.

LDC: Insert hook into middle horizontal bar of previous st, yo and pull up lp, insert hook in next ch or st, yo and pull up lp (3 lps on hook), [yo and draw through 2 lps] twice.

Directions

Note: Vest is worked in one piece to underarms, then divided into 3 sections for fronts and back. The only seam is at the shoulder. Blocking is important to eliminate curled edges of linked stitch.

BODY

With MC, ch 128 (140, 154, 168, 182).

Row 1 (RS) Insert hook in 2nd ch from hook, yo and pull up lp, skip 1 ch, [insert hook in next ch, yo and pull up lp] twice, [yo, draw through 2 lps] 3 times (beg LTR made), LTR in each ch across—124 (136, 150, 164, 178) LTR. Turn.

Row 2 Ch 1, working in front lps only, sc in each Linked st across, sc in top of beg ch. Turn.

Row 3 Ch 4, work beg LTR, LTR in each sc across. Turn.

Sizes M, L, XL and XXL only: Rep rows 2–3 (once, once, twice, twice).

Row 4 Ch 1, working in front lps only, sc in each Linked st across, join CC. Turn.

Row 5 Ch 3, work beg LDC, LDC in each sc across, break off CC, pu MC. Turn.

Rows 6–15 Rep rows 2–3 five times.

Rows 16–17 Rep rows 4–5.

Rows 18–25 Rep rows 2–3 four times.

Rows 26–27 Rep rows 4–5.

LEFT FRONT

Row 28 (WS) Ch 1, working in front lps only, sc in first 25 (28, 31, 35, 38) LDC, sc2tog. Turn, leaving rem sts unworked for back and right front.

Row 29 Ch 1, sc2tog, hdc in next sc, dc in next sc, tr in next sc, LTR in each sc to end. Turn.

Row 30 Ch 1, working in front lps only, sc in each LTR across, sc in tr—22 (25, 28, 32, 35) sts. Turn, leaving rem sts unworked.

Row 31 Rep row 3.

Rows 32–33 Rep rows 2–3.

Rows 34–35 Rep rows 4–5.

Rows 36–39 Rep rows 2–3 twice.

Rows 40–41 Rep rows 4–5.

Rows 42–43 Rep rows 2–3.

Sizes XL and XXL only: Rep rows 4–5 once, then rows 2–3 once.

Row 44 Rep row 4.

Shape Neck

Row 45 Ch 3, work beg LDC, LDC in next 11 (13, 16,

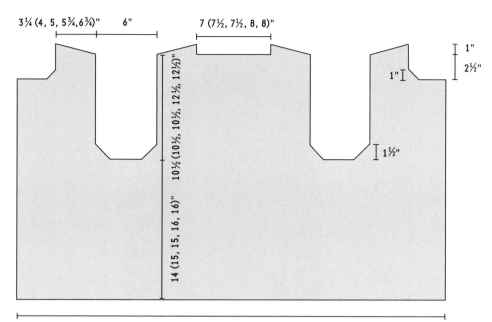

3¼ (4, 5, 5¾, 6¾)"   6"   7 (7½, 7½, 8, 8)"

1"
2½"
1"
1½"

10½ (10½, 10½, 12½, 12½)"

14 (15, 15, 16, 16)"

39 (43, 47, 51, 55)"

19, 22) sc, hdc in next sc, sc in next sc, sc2tog. Fasten off and turn, leaving rem sts unworked.

Row 46 Skip sc2tog, sc and hdc, join MC to first LDC. Ch 1, working in front lps only, sc in each LDC across— 11 (13, 16, 19, 22) sc. Turn.

Rows 47–49 Rep rows 3–5.

Shape Shoulder

Row 50 Ch 1, working in front lps only, sc in next 8 (10, 12, 15, 17) LTR. Turn.

Row 51 Ch 1, sl st in first 2 (3, 3, 4, 5) sc, sc in next 2 (3, 3, 4, 4) sc, hdc in next 2 (2, 3, 4, 4) sc, dc in last 2 (2, 3, 3, 4) sc. Fasten off.

BACK

With WS facing, skip 8 LDC from left front. Join MC to next LDC.

Row 28 Ch 1, sc2tog (in same LDC and next LDC),

working in front lps only, sc in next 50 (56, 64, 70, 78) LDC, sc2tog. Turn, leaving rem sts unworked for right front.

Row 29 Ch 1, sc2tog, hdc in next sc, dc in next sc, tr in next sc, LTR in 43 (49, 57, 63, 71) sc, dc in next sc, hdc in next sc, sc2tog. Fasten off and turn.

Row 30 Skip sc2tog, hdc and dc, join MC to first LTR, working in front lps only, sc in each LTR across, sc in tr—44 (50, 58, 64, 72) sc. Turn.

Row 31 Rep row 3.

Rows 32–33 Rep rows 2–3.

Rows 34–35 Rep rows 4–5.

Rows 36–39 Rep rows 2–3 twice.

Rows 40–41 Rep rows 4–5.

Rows 42–49 Rep rows 2–5 twice.

Sizes XL and XXL only: Rep rows 2–5 once.

Shape Left Shoulder

Row 50 Sl st in first 3 (3, 4, 4, 5) LTR, working in front lps only, sc in next 8 (10, 12, 15, 17) LTR. Turn.

Row 51 Ch 3, dc in next 2 (2, 3, 3, 4) sc, hdc in next 2 (2, 3, 4, 4) sc, sc in next 2 (3, 3, 4, 4) sc, sl st in last 2 (3, 3, 4, 5) sc. Fasten off.

Shape Right Shoulder

With WS facing, skip 22 (24, 24, 26, 26) LTR from left shoulder and join MC to next LTR.

Row 50 Ch 1, working in front lps only, sc in next 7 (9, 11, 14, 16) LTR. Turn.

Row 51 Sl st in first 2 (3, 3, 4, 5) sc, sc in next 2 (3, 3, 4, 4) sc, hdc in next 2 (2, 2, 3, 4, 4) sc, dc in last 2 (2, 3, 3, 4) sc. Fasten off.

RIGHT FRONT

With WS facing, skip 8 LDC from back. Join MC to next LDC.

Row 28 Ch 1, sc2tog (in same sc and next sc), working in front lps only, sc in each LDC across—26 (29, 32, 36, 39) sc. Turn.

Row 29 Ch 4, work beg LTR, LTR in next 20 (23, 26, 30, 33) sc, tr in next sc, dc in next sc, hdc in next sc, sc2tog. Fasten off and turn.

Row 30 Skip sc2tog, hdc and dc, join MC to tr, working in front lps only, sc in each LTR across—22 (25, 28, 32, 35) sc.

Row 31 Rep row 3.

Rows 32–33 Rep rows 2–3.

Rows 34–35 Rep rows 4–5.

Rows 36–39 Rep rows 2–3 twice.

Rows 40–41 Rep rows 4–5.

Rows 42–43 Rep rows 2–3.

Sizes XL and XXL only: Rep rows 4–5 once, then rows 2–3 once.

Row 44 Rep row 4.

Shape Neck

Row 45 Skip first 7 (8, 8, 9, 9) sc, join CC to next sc, sc2tog (in same sc and next sc), sc in next sc, hdc in next sc, dc in next sc, LDC in rem 10 (12, 15, 18, 21) sc. Join MC and turn.

Row 46 Ch 1, working in front lps only, sc in each LDC across, sc in dc—11 (13, 16, 19, 22) sc. Turn.

Row 47–49 Rep rows 3–5.

Shape Shoulder

Row 50 Ch 1, sl st in first 3 (3, 4, 4, 5) LTR, working in front lps only, sc in each LTR across—8 (10, 12, 15, 17) sc. Turn.

Row 51 Ch 3 (counts as 1 dc), dc in next 1 (1, 2, 2, 3) sc, hdc in next 2 (2, 3, 4, 4) sc, sc in next 2 (3, 3, 4, 4) sc, sl st in last 2 (3, 3, 4, 5) sc. Fasten off.

FINISHING

Block by laying vest flat on towel and pinning to measurements; spray lightly with water and allow to dry completely.

With RS tog, join shoulder seams using sl st.

Front Edging

With RS facing, join MC to bottom of front edge and sl st evenly up to neck opening. Fasten off. Rep on opposite side.

Chain Embellishment

With CC at WS of lower edge of left front, insert hook from RS to WS and pull up a lp, *with 1 lp on hook, insert hook approx ¼" above lp as before and pull up a lp through lp on hook; rep from * to top edge. Fasten off. Work another chain 1 st over.

Ribbing

With RS facing, join MC to underarm or bottom of front edge. Ch 5.

Row 1 Sc in 2nd ch from hook and in each ch across, sl st in next st of vest twice (first st joins row to vest, second st counts as turning ch). Turn.

Row 2 Working in back lps only, sc in each sc across. Turn.

Row 3 Ch 1, working in back lps only, sc in each sc across, sl st in next st of vest twice. Turn.

Rep rows 2–3 evenly around armholes and body. Fasten off. Whip stitch last row and foundation ch of armbands tog.

Collar

With RS facing, join MC to front neck edge. Ch 12.

Row 1 Sc in 2nd ch from hook and in each ch across, sl st in next st of vest twice (first st joins row to vest, second st counts as turning ch). Turn.

Row 2 Working in back lps only, sc in each sc across. Turn.

Row 3 Ch 1, working in back lps only, sc in each sc across, sl st in next st of vest twice. Turn.

Rep rows 2–3 evenly around neck opening. Fasten off.

Weave in ends.

Pin zipper into body opening. With sewing needle and thread, sew zipper in place using back st.

About Robyn My older sister used to tell everyone that I was going to have my own fashion line one day. Unfortunately, that only lasted until I enrolled in college as an architectural engineer. My day job is designing structural renovations and restorations of existing buildings, which may seem like a far cry from crochet fashion design. But for me, they are one and the same. They both use my ability to take a big project and break it down into small parts that I can understand, then piece them back together for the overall big picture. You can find more of my architecturally inspired pieces at my website, www.crochetbyfaye.com.

Size

S (M, L, XL)

Finished chest: 40 (43½, 46½, 50)"

Finished length: 25 (25, 26, 26)"

Materials

Brown Sheep *Nature Spun Sport* (100% wool; 50g/184 yd)

A: 3 (3, 3, 4) balls #N25 Enchanted Forest

B: 1 ball #522 Nervous Green

C: 1 ball #N24 Evergreen

D: 1 ball #N109 Spring Green

E: 1 (1, 2, 2) balls #740 Snow

US 5 (3.75mm) 32" and 16" circular needles, or sizes needed to obtain gauge

2 stitch markers

2 stitch holders

Crochet hook (E or F) for picking up sts

Gauge

24 sts and 28 rows = 4" in St st over chart patt

KIM HAMLIN

Anchors Aweigh

There's something innocent about the anchor. It reminds me of Fleet Week in NYC, when all these young sailors arrive on land, ready to take in the thrills of the big city and perhaps get a tattoo to serve as a reminder. Since anchors make me swoon, I designed this vest as a selfish way to see more dudes wearing them! I decided fresh green colors would be an exciting departure from the standard blue and white palette for this motif. I could also see it in gray stripes with exciting caution-yellow anchors. It takes a certain boldness to wear such a strong pattern, so you might tone it down by pairing the vest with a small-patterned casual shirt or a tweed sport coat. Knitting the vest is fun and easy, because it's knit in the round up to the armpits. The anchors are knit using the Fair Isle technique, simply carrying the unused strand behind the work and twisting it every five stitches. So even with all this color, you're only ever using two colors in a row!

Directions

Construction note: This vest is knit in the round to armhole. Unless noted, keep color chart patterning throughout.

Fair Isle note: Since white (color E) is used in most rows, carry it rather than cutting it, catching the yarn when it is not being used for more than 5 stitches.

BODY

With D and longer needle, CO 120 (130, 140, 150) sts, pm, CO 120 (130, 140, 150) sts—240 (260, 280, 300) sts. Pm and join.

Change to A. Work in k1, p1 rib for 2". K 5 rnds.

Work 36 rnds of chart until piece meas 15½ (15½, 16, 16)" from beg, ending 4 sts before end of last rnd.

Divide for front and back as foll: BO 8 sts, work to 4 sts before next marker, BO 8 sts, work to end—112 (122, 132, 142) sts each for front and back.

BACK

Work back and forth in chart patt, shaping armholes as foll:

Next row (WS) Purl.

Dec row K2, ssk, k to last 4 sts, k2tog, k2.

Rep last 2 rows 9 times more—92 (102, 112, 122) sts.

Cont even until armhole meas approx 9½ (9½, 10, 10)", ending with row 11, 23 or 35 of chart. BO.

FRONT

With WS facing, join yarn to front.

Work as for back until armhole meas 4", ending with a WS row.

K46 (51, 56, 61), turn. P to end.

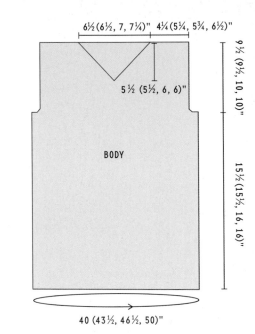

Left Shoulder

Dec row K to 4 sts from neck edge, k2tog, k2.

Next row Purl.

Rep last 2 rows 17 (16, 18, 19) times more— 28 (34, 37, 41) sts.

Next row Knit.

Next row Purl.

Dec row K to 4 sts from neck edge, k2tog, k2.

Next row Purl.

Rep last 4 rows 1 (2, 1, 1) times more—26 (31, 35, 39) sts.

Cont even in chart patt to match back. BO.

Right Shoulder

With WS facing, join yarn to right front and p 1 row.

Dec row K2, ssk, k to end.

Next row Purl.

Rep last 2 rows 17 (16, 18, 19) times more—28 (34, 37, 41) sts.

Next row Knit.

Next row Purl.

Next row K2, ssk, k to end.

Next row Purl.

Rep last 4 rows 1 (2, 1, 1) times more—26 (31, 35, 39) sts.

Cont even in chart patt to match left front. BO.

ARMHOLE BANDS

Sew shoulder seams.

With RS facing, A and shorter needle, starting at center of underarm, PU 114 (114, 120, 120) sts evenly around armhole. Pm and join.

Work in k1, p1 rib for 1".

Change to D and work 1 rnd rib. BO in rib.

Rep for other armhole.

NECKBAND

With RS facing, A and shorter needle, starting at base of V, PU 48 (50, 50, 52) sts along left front, 40 (40, 42, 44) sts across back and 48 (50, 50, 52) sts along right front—136 (140, 142, 148) sts.

Work back and forth in k1, p1 rib for 1".

Change to D and work 1 row rib. BO in rib.

FINISHING

Sew left side of V-neck edging over right side.

Using tapestry needle, weave in ends.

Block to measurements.

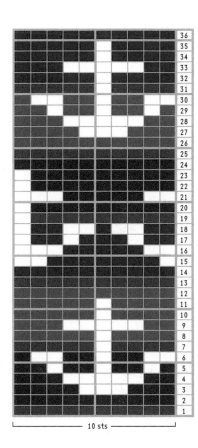

10 sts

■ A
■ B
■ C
■ D
☐ E

Smokin'

I've always been drawn to the classics—smoking jackets, cozy wool cardigans, and tweed in all forms. This pattern is a contemporary spin on an old standby, done up in a deep burgundy tweed, with large patch pockets to carry a pipe and glasses (or more fittingly, MP3 player, subway map, or cell phone), sophisticated leather buttons, and a classically indulgent shawl collar. It's just the type of thing he'll throw on while relaxing at the fireside with fresh coffee and a good book. Worked with chunky-weight wool in a slightly tighter gauge than usual, this jacketlike sweater knits up quickly and is sure to turn heads while keeping him warm and fashionable all winter.

Directions

Note: All parts of this sweater are worked in the round. Sleeves and body are worked from the bottom up separately to the armholes. At this point, the three pieces are joined together on one circular needle and the yoke is shaped as one piece toward the collar, using raglan shaping and finishing with a saddle-yoke shoulder treatment. The button band and shawl collar are worked last and seamed to the body in order to most accurately place buttonholes and ease in bands.

BODY

With circular needle, CO 146 (158, 170, 184, 196) sts.

Work back and forth in garter st (knit every row) for 1".

Work buttonhole as foll:

Size

S (M, L, XL, XXL)

Finished chest: 42½ (46, 50, 54, 58)"

Finished length: 28 (28, 28½, 29, 29½)"

Materials

Rowan *Scottish Tweed Chunky* (100% wool; 100g/109 yd), 10 (10, 11, 12, 13) balls #017 Lobster

US 10 (6mm) 40" circular needle, or size needed to obtain gauge

US 10 (6mm) double-pointed needles (set of 5)

Waste yarn

Stitch markers

Five 25mm leather-cased buttons

Sewing needle and matching thread

Gauge

13 sts and 23 rows = 4" in St st

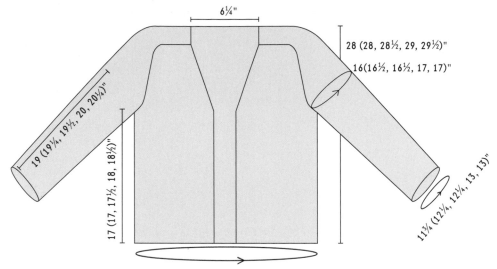

6¼"

28 (28, 28½, 29, 29½)"

16(16½, 16½, 17, 17)"

19 (19¼, 19½, 20, 20½)"

17 (17, 17½, 18, 18½)"

11¾ (12¼, 12¼, 13, 13)"

42½ (46, 50, 54, 58)"

Row 1 (RS) K to last 5 sts, BO 2 sts, k to end.

Row 2 K 3 sts, CO 2 sts, k to end.

Cont in garter st until body meas 3" from beg, ending with a WS row.

Next row K to last 8 sts and place those 8 sts onto wy.

Next row P to last 8 sts and place those 8 sts onto wy—130 (142, 154, 168, 180) sts.

These 8 sts from each edge of body will be picked up later for button bands.

Work even in St st until piece meas 17 (17, 17½, 18, 18½)" from beg, ending with a WS row. Do not break yarn. Set body aside and begin work on sleeves.

SLEEVES (MAKE 2)

CO 38 (40, 40, 42, 42) sts and divide evenly over 4 dpns. Pm and join.

Rnd 1 Knit.

Rnd 2 Purl.

Rep rnds 1 and 2 until sleeve meas 2½" from beg.

Work even in St st (knit all rnds) for 1½".

Inc rnd K1, m1, k to last st, m1, k1—40 (42, 42, 44, 44) sts.

Cont in St st, rep inc rnd every 11th rnd 6 times more— 52 (54, 54, 56, 56) sts.

Cont even in St st until sleeve meas 19 (19¼, 19½, 20, 20¼)" from beg, ending 5 (6, 6, 6, 7) sts before end of rnd. Place next 10 (12, 12, 12, 14) sts onto wy for underarm. Break off yarn, leaving an 18" tail for grafting.

Yoke Shaping

Set-up row (RS) K24 (26, 29, 33, 35) right front sts, pm, k1, pm, place next 10 (12, 12, 12, 14) sts onto wy for underarm, k42 (42, 42, 44, 42) sleeve sts, pm, k1, pm, k58 (62, 68, 74, 78) back sts, pm, k1, pm, place next 10 (12, 12, 12, 14) sts onto wy for underarm, k42 (42, 42, 44, 42) sleeve sts, pm, k1, pm, k24 (26, 29, 33, 35) left front sts—194 (202, 214, 232, 236) sts.

For sizes S, M, L, and XL, begin here. For size XXL, begin with row 9.

Rows 1, 3, 5, 7 and all WS rows Purl.

Rows 2 and 4 (RS) *K to 2 sts before next marker, ssk, k1, k2tog; rep from * 3 times more, k to end—8 sts decreased.

Row 6 *Size S only,* rep row 2. *All other sizes,* knit.

Row 8 K1, ssk, *k to 2 sts before next marker, ssk, k1, k2tog; rep from * 3 times more, k to last 3 sts, k2tog, k1—160 (176, 188, 206, —) sts.

Rows 9–11 Work even in St st, beg with a p row.

Row 12 *K to 2 sts before next marker, ssk, k1, k2tog; rep from * 3 times more, k to end—8 sts decreased.

Rows 13–15 Work even in St st.

Row 16 K1, ssk, *k to 2 sts before next marker, ssk, k1, k2tog; rep from * 3 times more, k to last 3 sts, k2tog, k1—10 sts decreased.

Rep rows 9–16 three (three, four, four, five) times more, then rows 9–12 once (once, 0, 0, once) more—80 (96, 98, 116, 128) sts: 6 (9, 10, 14, 17) sts on right and left fronts, 16 (18, 16, 18, 18) sleeve sts, 32 (38, 42, 48, 54) back sts and 4 seam sts.

Saddle Shoulder Shaping
Right shoulder

Set-up row (partial) K7 (10, 11, 15, 18)—right front plus 1 seam st. Do not turn.

Row 1 (RS) Cont over sleeve sts, sl 1, k14 (16, 14, 16, 16), ssk (working last sleeve st tog with first back st [seam st on very first row]). Turn.

Row 2 (WS) Sl 1, p14 (16, 14, 16, 16), p2tog (working last sleeve st tog with 1 front st). Turn.

Rep rows 1 and 2 until all sts of right front have been worked, ending with a WS row.

Back right shoulder

Set-up row (partial) BO 7 (8, 7, 8, 8) sts.

Row 1 (RS) K to last sleeve st, ssk (working last sleeve st tog with first back st). Turn.

Row 2 (WS) Sl 1, p6 (7, 6, 7, 7). Turn.

Rep rows 1 and 2 until you have reached center back neck.

Place rem 7 (8, 7, 8, 8) sts onto holder.

Left shoulder

Set-up row (partial) With WS facing, join yarn to left front edge. P7 (10, 11, 15, 18)—left front plus 1 seam st. Do not turn.

Row 1 (WS) Cont over sleeve sts, sl 1, p14 (16, 14, 16, 16), p2tog (working last sleeve st tog with first back st). Turn.

Row 2 (RS) Sl 1, k14 (16, 14, 16, 16), ssk (working last sleeve st tog with first front st). Turn.

Rep rows 1 and 2 until all sts of front have been worked, ending with a RS row.

Back left shoulder

Set-up row (partial) BO 7 (8, 7, 8, 8) sts pwise.

Row 1 (WS) P to last sleeve st, p2tog (working last sleeve st tog with first back st). Turn.

Row 2 (WS) Sl 1, k6 (7, 6, 7, 7). Turn.

Rep rows 1 and 2 until you have reached center back neck.

Using kitchener st, graft sts from each saddle tog.

FRONT BANDS & COLLAR
Right Button Band

Place 8 sts of right front band onto needle. With WS facing, join yarn. Work even in garter st until slightly stretched band reaches beg of neck shaping, ending with a WS row. Note the number of rows or ridges to determine buttonhole spacing on left band.

Shape Shawl Collar (Right Side)

Inc row (RS) K to last st, m1, k1.

Rep inc row every 6th row until there are 20 sts.

Work even in garter st until slightly stretched collar reaches center of right shoulder saddle, ending with a WS row.

Short Row Shaping

Row 1 K3, W&T.

Row 2 and all even rows Knit back.

Row 3 K6, W&T.

Row 5 K9, W&T.

Row 7 K12, W&T.

Row 9 K15, W&T.

Row 11 K18, W&T.

Row 13 K20.

Row 15 K18, W&T.

Row 17 K15, W&T.

Row 19 K12, W&T.

Row 21 K9, W&T.

Row 23 K6, W&T.

Row 25 K3, W&T.

Rows 27 and 28 K20.

Rep rows 1–28 once more.

Work even in garter st until slightly stretched collar reaches center back neck. Place sts on holder.

Left Buttonhole Band

Using number of rows noted from length of button band, determine how frequently you will need to work the four evenly spaced additional buttonholes along band.

Place sts of left band onto needle. With RS facing, join yarn. Work even in garter st until slightly stretched band reaches beg of neck shaping, working buttonholes where determined as foll:

Row 1 K3, BO 2 sts, k to end.

Row 2 K3, CO 2 sts, k to end.

Shape Shawl Collar (Left Side)

Inc row (WS) K to last st, m1, k1.

Rep inc row every 6th row until there are 20 sts.

Work even in garter st until collar reaches center of left shoulder saddle, ending with a RS row.

Work short row shaping same as for Right Side (row 1 will be a WS row).

Using 3-needle BO, join 2 ends of shawl collar at center back neck.

POCKETS (MAKE 2)

CO 22 sts.

Work even in St st for 4¼". Work in Garter st for 1¾". BO.

Sew one pocket to each front, referring to photo for placement.

FINISHING

Sew button bands and collar to sweater body. Using sewing needle and thread, sew buttons to right front opposite buttonholes. Weave in ends.

Block sweater to measurements.

About Jared I am an artist, photographer, and knitwear designer based in Brooklyn, NY, though originally I hie from the Pacific Northwest, where I went to the University of Puget Sound in Tacoma, WA. Currently pursuing a master of fine arts at the New York Academy of Art, I continue to work as a freelance photographer and knitwear designer. Although I learned to knit as a child, it was only about five years ago that I became serious (obsessive) about this art form. I track my fiber-related exploits and satisfy my unreasonably voracious cravings for wool at www.brooklyntweed.net. Stop by and say hello!

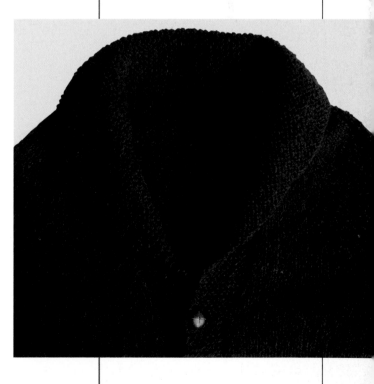

Size

S (M, L, XL, XXL)

Finished chest: 38 (42, 46, 50, 54)"

Finished length: 25 (25¾, 26¾, 27½, 28¼)"

Materials

MC: Noro *Silk Garden* (45% silk, 45% kid mohair, 10% lambswool; 50g/110 yd), 7 (8, 9, 10, 11) skeins #47

CC: Fable Handknit Pure Baby Alpaca (100% baby alpaca; 50g/145 yd), 6 (7, 7, 8, 8) skeins #07 black

US 9 (5.5mm) circular needle and dpns (set of 5)

US 10 (6mm) circular needle, or size needed to obtain gauge

3 stitch markers

4 stitch holders or waste yarn

Gauge

14 sts and 20 rows = 4" in St st with MC and CC held tog and larger needles

LAUREN LAX
Mixology

Alpaca, silk, kid mohair, and wool—did my boyfriend deserve such a special sweater? Yes, but I needed to make sure it was a sweater he'd love to wear—and that I'd love to make. The luxurious, variegated yarn will keep the knitter interested, while mixing it together with a strand of neutral black alpaca tones down the color changes, making it more suitable for a guy. The set-in sleeves are knit from the top down, so he can try it on as you knit and ensure the sleeve length is perfect. And the neckband is knit in ribbing, then doubled and sewn down on the inside to keep it nice and snug without being too tight. This sweater says thank you for all those visits to yarn shops and times he had to wait "just one more row."

Directions

Note: The only sewing involved in this pattern is securing the neckband to the inside of the sweater. The body is knit bottom-up in one piece, and the set-in sleeves are knit top down. Shoulders are short-rowed and joined with a 3 needle bind-off. Entire sweater is knit with the yarns held together.

BODY

With smaller needles and MC and CC held tog, CO 132 (148, 160, 176, 188) sts. Pm and join.

Work in k2, p2 rib for 2 (2, 2, 2¼, 2½)".

Change to larger needles and work even in St st until work meas 15½ (16, 16½, 16¾, 17)" from beg.

Divide for Front and Back.

BACK

BO 4 (5, 5, 6, 7) sts (1 st on RH needle), k next 61 (68, 74, 81, 86) sts, turn. BO 4 (5, 5, 6, 7) sts, p to end— 58 (64, 70, 76, 80) back sts.

Armhole Shaping

Next row (RS) K1, ssk, k to last 3 sts, k2tog, k1.

Next row Purl.

Rep last 2 rows 3 (3, 4, 5, 5) times more—50 (56, 60, 64, 68) sts.

Cont even in St st until armholes meas 8½ (8¾, 9¼, 9¾, 10¼)", ending with a WS row.

Neck Shaping (Right Side)

Row 1 (RS) K17 (20, 22, 23, 25), turn.

Row 2 BO 2 (2, 3, 3, 4) sts, p to end.

Row 3 Knit.

Row 4 BO 1 (2, 2, 2, 2) sts, p to end—14 (16, 17, 18, 19) sts on right shoulder.

Work even until armhole meas 9½ (9¾, 10¼, 10¾, 11¼)", ending with a RS row.

Shoulder Shaping (Right Side)

Next row (WS) P to last 7 (8, 8, 9, 9) sts, W&T.

Next row K to end.

Next row Purl, picking up wrap and p tog with wrapped st. Place 14 (16, 17, 18, 19) sts on holder or wy.

Neck Shaping (Left Side)

Place center 16 (16, 16, 18, 18) sts on holder or wy.

With WS facing, join yarns to sts of left side.

Row 1 (WS) P17 (20, 22, 23, 25).

Row 2 BO 2 (2, 3, 3, 4) sts, k to end.

Row 3 Purl.

Row 4 BO 1 (2, 2, 2, 2) sts, k to end—14 (16, 17, 18, 19) sts on left shoulder.

Work even until armhole meas same as right side, ending with a WS row.

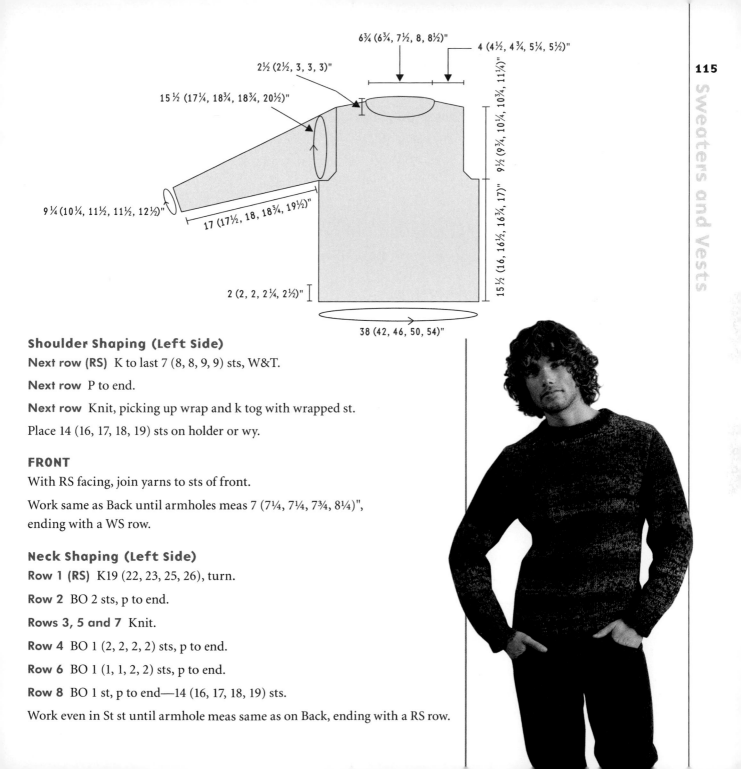

6¾ (6¾, 7½, 8, 8½)"

4 (4½, 4¾, 5¼, 5½)"

2½ (2½, 3, 3, 3)"

15 ½ (17¼, 18¾, 18¾, 20½)"

9¼ (10¼, 11½, 11½, 12½)"

17 (17½, 18, 18¾, 19½)"

9½ (9¾, 10¼, 10¾, 11¼)"

15 ½ (16, 16½, 16¾, 17)"

2 (2, 2, 2¼, 2½)"

38 (42, 46, 50, 54)"

Shoulder Shaping (Left Side)

Next row (RS) K to last 7 (8, 8, 9, 9) sts, W&T.

Next row P to end.

Next row Knit, picking up wrap and k tog with wrapped st.

Place 14 (16, 17, 18, 19) sts on holder or wy.

FRONT

With RS facing, join yarns to sts of front.

Work same as Back until armholes meas 7 (7¼, 7¼, 7¾, 8¼)", ending with a WS row.

Neck Shaping (Left Side)

Row 1 (RS) K19 (22, 23, 25, 26), turn.

Row 2 BO 2 sts, p to end.

Rows 3, 5 and 7 Knit.

Row 4 BO 1 (2, 2, 2, 2) sts, p to end.

Row 6 BO 1 (1, 1, 2, 2) sts, p to end.

Row 8 BO 1 st, p to end—14 (16, 17, 18, 19) sts.

Work even in St st until armhole meas same as on Back, ending with a RS row.

Shoulder Shaping (Left Side)

Work same as Back shoulder shaping (right side).

Neck Shaping (Right Side)

Place center 12 (12, 14, 14, 16) sts on holder or wy.

With WS facing, join yarns to sts of right side.

Row 1 (WS) P19 (22, 23, 25, 26).

Row 2 BO 2 sts, k to end.

Rows 3, 5 and 7 Purl.

Row 4 BO 1 (2, 2, 2, 2) sts, k to end.

Row 6 BO 1 (1, 1, 2, 2) sts, k to end.

Row 8 BO 1 st, k to end—14 (16, 17, 18, 19) sts.

Work even in St st until armhole meas same as left side, ending with a WS row.

Shoulder Shaping (Right Side)

Work same as Back shoulder shaping (left side).

SLEEVES (MAKE 2)

Join shoulder sts using 3-needle BO.

With RS facing and starting at RH edge of BO underam sts, PU and k4 (5, 5, 6, 7), pm A, PU and k4 (5, 5, 6, 7), pm B, PU and k46 (50, 56, 54, 58) sts evenly around rem of armhole—54 (60, 66, 66, 72) sts. Pm C and join.

Row 1 K32 (35, 39, 38, 41) sts past B, W&T.

Row 2 P18 (20, 22, 22, 24), W&T.

Row 3 K19 (21, 23, 23, 25), picking up wraps and k tog with wrapped st, W&T.

Row 4 P20 (22, 24, 24, 26), picking up wraps and p tog with wrapped st, W&T.

Cont as est, working 1 more st before W&T each row and working wraps tog with wrapped st until you reach C.

Next rnd Knit, removing markers B and C, and working rem wraps tog with wrapped sts—54 (60, 63, 69, 72) sts. Marker A should be at center of underarm, beg of rnd.

K 5 rnds.

Dec rnd K1, ssk, k to last 3 sts, k2tog, k1.

Rep dec rnd every 6th rnd until 32 (36, 40, 40, 44) sts rem.

Work even in St st until sleeve meas 15 (15½, 16, 16½, 17)" from underarm or 2 (2, 2, 2¼, 2½)" less than desired finished length.

Cuff

Change to smaller needles and work in k2, p2 rib for 2 (2, 2, 2¼, 2½)". BO loosely in rib.

NECKBAND

With RS facing and smaller needle, starting at left shoulder seam, PU and k10 (10, 10, 10, 11) sts down left front neck, k12 (12, 14, 14, 16) sts across center front, PU and k10 (10, 10, 10, 11) sts up right front neck, PU and k6 (6, 7, 6, 6) sts down right back neck, k16 (16, 16, 18, 18) center back sts, PU and k6 (6, 7, 6, 6) sts up left back neck—60 (60, 64, 64, 68) sts. Pm and join.

Work in k2, p2 rib until neckband measures 3". BO loosely in rib. Break yarns, leaving a 30" tail. Fold neckband to inside of garment and sew BO edge to PU edge. Weave in ends.

About Lauren When I learned to knit in 1999, I knew no other knitters and had to buy yarn from places that also sold dog food and electric drills. I'm grateful for all the knitters I have met in person and online since then and for the chance to work with some of the most luscious yarns around. I would rather keep my boyfriend warm than let a superstition dictate my knitting, so when he arrived at Yale from L.A., with few sweaters and no hats, scarves, or wool socks, I immediately set about changing that. We have recently moved from Connecticut to California, and I am adjusting to the warmer weather— and the diminished need for heavy sweaters. When I'm not knitting, I can be found teaching math and economics and playing pub trivia.

KIM RUSSO

High-Top Hoodie

These days, everyone's into wearing hoodies, especially men. I really liked the contrasting colors of the stripes on the athletic styles and thought that would translate well to a knit pattern. This version is done in the contemporary color scheme of orange, brown, and tan, but feel free to incorporate the colors of his favorite sports team or school to make it personal for him. Although the raglan hoodie is usually a casual piece of clothing, when knit as a sweater it becomes a dressier garment. The wool yarn makes it warmer than a regular cotton hoodie, and if you layer it with a turtleneck or a T-shirt underneath, it's perfect for cool days outdoors. It's an unfussy design that even the choosiest of men won't object to and will wear over and over again.

Special technique

Crochet Provisional Cast-On
Using crochet hook, make a chain that's a few stitches longer than the required number of CO stitches. Break yarn and pull long loop through last chain. Insert knitting needle into the purl bump in back of first chain, wrap yarn and pull up a stitch. Rep in next chain and continue until required number of stitches are cast on.

Size

S (M, L, XL, XXL)

Finished chest: 40 (44, 48, 52, 56)"

Finished length: 28 (29¼, 30¼, 31, 32¾)"

Materials

Brown Sheep *Lamb's Pride Worsted* (85% wool, 15% mohair; 113g/190 yd)

MC: 4 (4, 5, 6, 6) skeins #M89 Roasted Coffee

CC1: 4 (5, 5, 6, 6) skeins #M22 Autumn Harvest

CC2: 1 (1, 1, 1, 1) skein #M115 Oatmeal

US 7 (4.5mm) 40" circular knitting needle, or size needed to obtain gauge

US 4 (3.5mm) 16" circular knitting needle

Stitch markers

Waste yarn

Size G/6 (4mm) crochet hook

Gauge

19 sts and 26 rows = 4" in St st

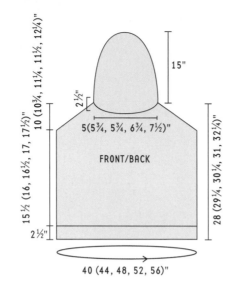

15"

2½"

5(5¾, 5¾, 6¾, 7½)"

FRONT/BACK

15½ (16, 16½, 17, 17½)"

10 (10¾, 11¼, 11½, 12¼)"

28 (29¼, 30¼, 31, 32¼)"

2½"

40 (44, 48, 52, 56)"

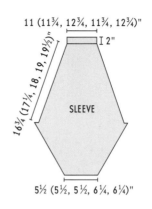

11 (11¾, 12¾, 11¾, 12¾)"

2"

SLEEVE

16¾ (17¼, 18, 19, 19½)"

5½ (5½, 5½, 6¼, 6¼)"

Directions

Note: The body of this pattern is knit in the round, with the raglan portions knit flat. The sleeves are knit from the top down and then sewn into the body. The hood is knit after the body and sleeves have been sewn together. The stripes for the sleeves and hood are added using a crochet hook after they have been knit.

BODY

With larger needle and MC, using the long-tail CO method, CO 94 (106, 114, 124, 132) sts, pm, CO 94 (106, 114, 124, 132) sts—188 (212, 228, 248, 264) sts. Pm and join.

Work in k2, p2 rib for 2½".

Work in St st until body meas 15½ (16, 16½, 17, 17½)" from beg, ending 5 (5, 5, 7, 7) sts before end of last rnd.

Divide for front and back as foll: BO 10 (10, 10, 14, 14) sts, work to 5 (5, 5, 7, 7) sts before next marker, BO 10 (10, 10, 14, 14) sts, work to end of rnd—84 (96, 104, 110, 118) sts each for front and back.

BACK

Next row (WS) Purl.

Raglan Shaping

Row 1 (RS) K2, ssk, k to last 4 sts, k2tog, k2.

Row 2 Purl.

Rep last 2 rows until 24 (28, 28, 32, 36) sts rem. Break yarn and place sts on wy.

FRONT

With WS facing, join yarn to front.

Next row (WS) Purl.

Work raglan shaping as for back until 42 (50, 58, 60, 64) sts rem, ending with a WS row.

Beg neck shaping while cont raglan shaping as foll:

Next row (RS) K2, ssk, k12 (13, 13, 15, 16), BO center 10 (10, 10, 12, 12) sts, k to last 4 sts, k2tog, k2— 16 (20, 24, 24, 26) sts each side. Work each side of neck separately.

Neck (Right Side)

Row 1 (WS) Purl.

Row 2 BO 2 sts at neck edge, k to last 4 sts, k2tog, k2—13 (17, 21, 21, 23) sts.

Row 3 Purl.

Rep rows 2 and 3 once (twice, twice, twice, 4 times) more—10 (11, 15, 15, 11) sts.

Next row BO 1 st at neck edge, k to last 4 sts, k2tog, k2—8 (9, 12, 12, 9) sts.

Next row Purl.

Rep last 2 rows twice (twice, twice, 3 times, once) more.

Cont dec as est at raglan edge only until 1 st rem.

Break yarn and place st on wy.

Neck (Left Side)

With WS facing, join yarn to sts of left side.

Row 1 (WS) Purl.

Row 2 K2, ssk, k to end.

Row 3 BO 2 sts at neck edge, p to end—13 (17, 21, 21, 23) sts.

Rep rows 2 and 3 once (twice, twice, twice, 4 times) more—10 (11, 15, 15, 11) sts.

Next row K2, ssk, k to end.

Next row BO 1 st at neck edge, p to end—8 (9, 12, 12, 9) sts.

Rep last 2 rows twice (twice, twice, 3 times, once) more.

Cont dec as est at raglan edge until only 1 st rem.

Break yarn and place st on wy.

SLEEVES (MAKE 2)

With CC1 and using crochet provisional CO method, CO 26 (26, 26, 30, 30) sts.

Row 1 K10 (10, 10, 12, 12), p2, k2, p2, k10 (10, 10, 12, 12).

Row 2 P10 (10, 10, 12, 12,), p2, k2, p2, k10 (10, 10, 12, 12,).

Row 3 (inc) K2, kfb, patt as est to last 3 sts, kfb, k2—28 (28, 28, 32, 32)sts.

Row 4 and every even row Work even in patt as est.

Rep inc row every RS row until there are 86 (94, 102, 108, 112) sts.

About Kim I'm thirty-two and live in Rockford, IL. I first picked up the needles at the age of eight, when my mother taught me the basics. Through the years, various events have prompted me to pick them up again, but it wasn't until my third child was in diapers that I began to take it seriously. The cloth diapers my son wore prompted me to try to knit wool soaker covers for him, and a serious obsession was born. After a few years as a professional knitter selling wool soakers, I decided to branch out to other items. Now I design, dye, and knit for my online boutique, www.KimberlyR.com. Part of my motivation is to lure people away from mass-manufactured products by showing them the quality of handmade goods.

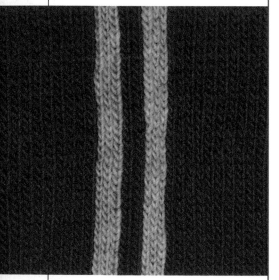

Next row BO 5 (5, 5, 7, 7) sts, cont in patt as est to end— 81 (89, 97, 101, 105) sts.

Next row BO 5 (5, 5, 7, 7) sts, cont in patt as est to end— 76 (84, 92, 94, 98) sts.

Work even in patt for 9 rows, ending on WS row.

Next row (dec) K1, ssk, patt as est to last 3 sts, k2tog, k1—74 (82, 90, 92, 96) sts.

Rep dec row every 10th row 7 (6, 2, 3, 2) times—60 (70, 86, 86, 92) sts.

Rep dec row every 8th row 2 (0, 4, 4, 4) times—56 (70, 78, 78, 84) sts.

Rep dec row every 6th row 2 (7, 9, 6, 8) times—52 (56, 60, 66, 68) sts.

Rep dec row every 4th row 0 (0, 0, 3, 4) times—52 (56, 60, 60, 60) sts.

Cuff

Change to smaller needle.

Row 1 P1, *k2, p2; rep from * to last st, p1.

Row 2 K1, *p2, k2; rep from * to last st, k1.

Rep last 2 rows until cuff meas 2". BO loosely.

Stripes

Create 3 rows of stripes by crocheting 3 chain rows in each column of purl stitches on each sleeve as follows: Starting at the top with CC2 underneath and RS facing, insert the crochet hook into the first p st and pull up a lp of CC2 to the RS. *With the lp on the hook, insert hook into the next row and pull up a lp of CC2 to the RS and through the lp on the hook; rep from * to beg of cuff. Break yarn, draw end through lp and secure. Rep twice more in same purl column and three times in 2nd purl column. Rep on other sleeve.

Sew sleeves to body of sweater. Sew underarm seams.

HOOD

Starting at right neck edge, place sts onto larger needle (pulling out provisional crochet ch from sleeve tops to release "live" sts) as foll: 1 st of right front, 26 (26, 26, 30, 30) sleeve sts, 24 (28, 28, 32, 36) back sts, 26 (26, 26, 30, 30) sleeve sts, 1 st of left front—78 (82, 82, 94, 98) sts.

With WS facing, join CC1.

Row 1 (WS) P11 (11, 11, 13, 13), k2, p2, k2, p44 (48, 48, 56, 60), k2, p2, k2, p11 (11, 11, 13, 13).

Row 2 Keeping in sleeve patt as est, k, inc 20 sts evenly across—98 (102, 102, 114, 118) sts.

Cont in St st and sleeve patt as est until hood meas 16". Divide sts evenly over 2 needles and fold hood lengthwise with RS tog. Seam top of hood using 3-needle BO. Work stripes on hood as for sleeves.

Ribbing

With RS facing, larger needle and CC1, starting at base of hood, PU a multiple of 4 sts evenly around edge of hood and across front neck. Pm and join. Work in k2, p2 rib for 1½". Break yarn and weave in ends.

FINISHING

Weave in ends and block pieces to measurements.

Size

S (M, L, XL, XXL)

Finished chest: 40 (44, 48, 52, 56)"

Finished length: 25 (26, 26½, 27, 27½)"

Materials

Reynolds *Andean Alpaca Regal* (90% Peruvian alpaca/10% wool; 100g/110 yd)

MC: 9 (11, 12, 13, 14) balls #42 Jeans

CC1: 1 ball #24 Brick

CC2: 2 balls #06 Off-White

Size US 10 (6mm) straight needles and 16" circular needle, or size needed to obtain gauge

Stitch markers

Gauge

16 sts and 20 rows = 4" in St st

DEBBIE STOLLER

High Fidelity

He can rock two turntables and a microphone in this modern take on the old-school ski sweater. Made in an ultra-luxurious alpaca-blend yarn, in the traditional colors of navy blue, red, and white, the 45-record adapters that appear in a wide stripe across the chest and upper arms look at first glance like snowflakes, but they are so much cooler. A nice, loose fit makes it comfy and cozy—perfect for lounging around with a stack of LPs, or even hitting the slopes. So bust out the old singles, crank up the hi-fi, and get ready to make some noise.

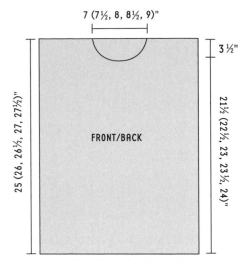

7 (7½, 8, 8½, 9)"

3½"

FRONT/BACK

25 (26, 26½, 27, 27½)"

21½ (22½, 23, 23½, 24)"

20½ (22½, 24½, 26½, 28½)"

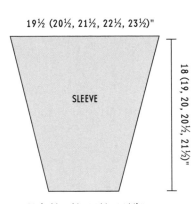

19½ (20½, 21½, 22½, 23½)"

SLEEVE

18 (19, 20, 20½, 21½)"

8½ (8½, 9½, 10½, 10½)"

Directions

BACK

Using MC, CO 82 (90, 98, 106, 114) sts.

Work in k1, p1 rib for 1½", ending with a WS row.

Work in St st until piece meas 13¾ (14¼, 14½, 14¾, 15)", ending with a WS row.

Work 3 rows of Chart A.

With MC, p 1 row.

Work 14 rows of Chart B, beg at st 2 (12, 8, 4, 14) and ending last rep at st 13 (3, 7, 11, 1).

With MC, k 1 row.

Work 3 rows of Chart A.

Cont in St st with MC until piece meas 25 (26, 26½, 27, 27½)" from beg, ending with a WS row.

BO 27 (30, 33, 36, 39) sts, k28 (30, 32, 34, 36) sts, BO rem 27 (30, 33, 36, 39) sts. Place center 28 (30, 32, 34, 36) sts on holder for back neck.

FRONT

Work same as for back until piece meas 21½ (22½, 23, 23½, 24)" from beg, ending with a WS row.

Next row K34 (37, 41, 44, 48), BO 14 (16, 16, 18, 18) sts, k to end.

Working both sides at the same time, BO 1 st at neck edge every other row 7 (7, 8, 8, 9) times—27 (30, 33, 36, 39) sts each shoulder. Cont even in St st until front meas same as back. BO.

SLEEVES (MAKE 2)

Using MC, CO 34 (34, 38, 42, 42) sts.

Work in k1, p1 rib for 1½", ending with a WS row.

Cont in St st, inc 1 st each side on next and every other row 6 (7, 5, 5, 6) times total, then every 4th row 16 (17, 19, 19, 20) times—78 (82, 86, 90, 94) sts.

AT THE SAME TIME, when sleeve meas 12½ (13½, 14½, 15, 16)" from beg, ending with a WS row:

Work 3 rows Chart A.

Chart A

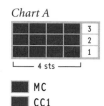

├─ 4 sts ─┤

■ MC
■ CC1

Chart B

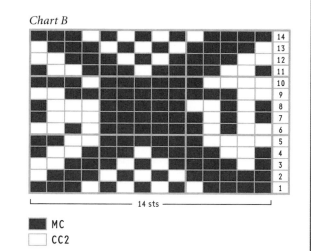

├───── 14 sts ─────┤

■ MC
□ CC2

With MC, p 1 row.

Work 14 rows Chart B, beg with st 1 for all sizes.

With MC, k 1 row.

Work 3 rows Chart A.

Cont even in St st with MC until piece meas 18 (19, 20, 20½, 21½)" from beg. BO.

FINISHING
Sew shoulder seams.

Neckband
Slip 28 (30, 32, 34, 36) sts from holder onto circular needle, PU and k36 (40, 44, 46, 50) sts evenly around front neck—64 (70, 76, 80, 86) sts. Pm and join. Work in k1, p1 rib for 1". BO loosely in rib.

Pm at front and back side edges 9¾ (10¼, 10¾, 11¼, 11¾)" down from shoulder seams. Sew sleeves to body between markers, matching center of sleeves to shoulder seams. Sew sleeve and side seams. Weave in ends.

ADRIAN BIZILIA

Biker Boy

My husband, who was a bike messenger in Boston for many years, was an expert on what made a good layering sweater. It had to have a full zip for easy removal, long and slim arms so that his wrists were covered, and a long enough body so that no matter how far he leaned over, his lower back was never exposed. I noticed that his sweater would pill and wear where the strap of his messenger bag sat on his shoulder, so I included a removable patch for protection. (The patch can always be replaced.) This Biker sweater is quite fitted. If you'd like a more traditional sweater fit, go up an inch or two in circumference, although note that the length of the sleeves will grow ¼" for every inch added to the sweater circumference. Since the sleeves are designed to be long to begin with, you may want to subtract a bit of length somewhere between the elbow and underarm.

Directions

Note: This sweater is knit from the bottom up with a collar lining knit up from the collar, then folded over and sewn down after the zipper is sewn in. The sleeves are knit flat to the end of the vertical stripe section, then joined and knit in the round to the underarm. The body is knit flat to the underarm, and then joined with the arms and knit flat. Circular needles are called for because they are better at supporting the weight of a whole sweater, easing wrist strain.

Size

S (M, L, XL, XXL)

Finished chest: 38 (40, 44, 48, 52)"

Finished length: 24½ (25½, 26½, 27¾, 29)"

Materials

Peace Fleece *Worsted Weight* (30% mohair, 70% wool; 113g/200 yd)

MC: 6 (6, 7, 7, 8) skeins Baku Black

CC: 1 skein Fathers Gray

Collar lining: Knit Picks *Ambrosia* (80% alpaca, 20% cashmere; 50g/110 yd), 1 skein Fog

US 4 (3.5mm) 24" circular needle

US 6 (4mm) 16" and 24" circular needles, or size needed to obtain gauge

4 stitch holders or waste yarn

4 stitch markers

24 (25, 27, 28, 29)" separating zipper (Buy zipper after you've finished sweater and measured opening. Any gauge change will change zipper length needed.)

Sewing needle and matching thread

Straight pins, for zipper and patch placement

Gauge

16 sts and 24 rows = 4" in St st

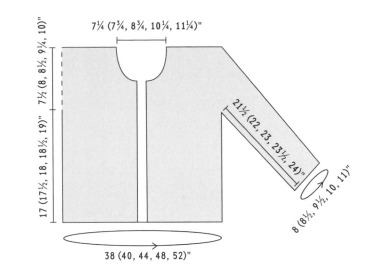

7¼ (7¾, 8¾, 10¼, 11¼)"

7½ (8, 8½, 9¼, 10)"

17 (17½, 18, 18½, 19)"

21½ (22, 23, 23½, 24)"

8 (8½, 9½, 10, 11)"

38 (40, 44, 48, 52)"

BODY

With smaller needle and CC, CO 153 (161, 177, 193, 209) sts.

Row 1 (WS) Sl 1 kwise, *k1, p1; rep from * to last 2 sts, k2.

Row 2 Sl 1 kwise, k1, *k1, p1; rep from * to last 3 sts, k3.

Break yarn and change to MC.

Rows 3–14 Rep rows 1 and 2.

Change to 24" larger needle.

Row 1 Sl 1 kwise, k to end.

Row 2 Sl 1 kwise, k1, p to last 2 sts, k2.

Rep last 2 rows until body meas 17 (17½, 18, 18½, 19)" from beg, ending with a WS row. Do not break yarn. Leave on needle and set aside.

SLEEVES (MAKE TWO)

With smaller needle and MC, CO 23 (25, 29, 31, 35) sts; change to CC and CO 9 sts—32 (34, 38, 40, 44) sts. Work in rib, keeping in color patt, as foll:

Row 1 (RS) K1, *k1, p1; rep from * to last st, k1.

Row 2 P1, *k1, p1; rep from * to end, p1.

Rep last 2 rows 6 times more.

Change to 16" larger needle. Work in St st, cont in color patt as est.

Inc row (RS) K1, kfb, k to last 2 MC sts, kfb, k1, k to end in CC.

Cont in St st in color patt as est, rep inc row every 6th row 9 (10, 10, 12, 12) times more—52 (56, 60, 66, 70) sts, ending with a WS row.

Break off CC and work remainder of sleeve in MC.

Pm and join.

Next rnd K2tog tbl, k to last 2 sts, k2tog—50 (54, 58, 64, 68) sts.

Cont even in St st until sleeve meas 21½ (22, 23, 23½, 24)" from beg, ending 6 sts before end of rnd. Place next 12 sts onto wy for underarm.

JOIN SLEEVES TO BODY

Joining rnd (RS) Sl 1 kwise, k31 (33, 37, 41, 45) right front sts, place next 12 sts onto wy for underarm, pm, k38 (42, 46, 52, 56) sleeve sts, pm, k65 (69, 77, 85, 93) back sts, place next 12 sts onto wy for underarm, pm, k38 (42, 46, 52, 56) sleeve sts, pm, k32 (34, 38, 42, 46) left front sts—205 (221, 245, 273, 297) sts.

Next row (WS) Sl 1 kwise, k1, p to last 2 sts, k2.

Cont in St st with sl st garter st edge as est for 1½", ending with a WS row.

Raglan Shaping

Dec row 1 (RS) Sl 1 kwise, *k to 2 sts from marker, k2tog, sm, ssk; rep from * 3 times more, k to end—197 (213, 237, 265, 289) sts.

Next row Sl 1 kwise, k1, p to last 2 sts, k2.

Rep last 2 rows 12 times more, ending with a WS row—101 (117, 141, 169, 193) sts; 19 (21, 25, 29, 33) sts in each front.

Patch Chart

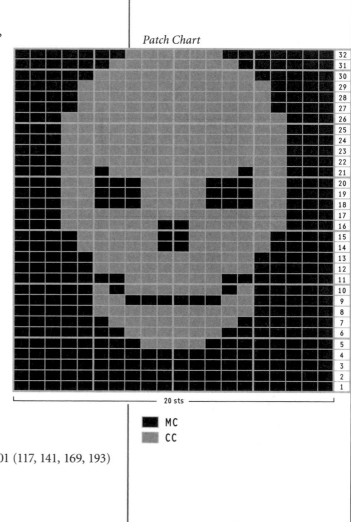

20 sts

32
31
30
29
28
27
26
25
24
23
22
21
20
19
18
17
16
15
14
13
12
11
10
9
8
7
6
5
4
3
2
1

■ MC
▨ CC

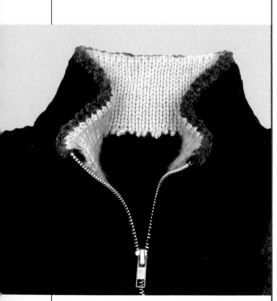

Neck Shaping

Cont dec as est, BO 6 sts at beg of next 2 rows—81 (97, 121, 149, 173) sts; 12 (14, 18, 22, 26) sts in each front.

Row 1 (RS) K1, ssk, *k to 2 sts from marker, k2tog, sm, ssk; rep from * 3 times more, k to last 3 sts, k2tog, k1.

Row 2 Purl.

Rep last 2 rows 3 (4, 6, 8, 10) times more—41 (47, 51, 59, 63) sts; 4 sts in each front.

Size S only (RS): Ssk, k2tog, sm, k2, sm, ssk, k to 2 sts from next marker, k2tog, sm, k2, ssk, k2tog—35 sts.

Sizes M, L, XL and XXL only (RS): Ssk, k2tog, sm, *ssk, k to 2 sts from marker, k2tog, sm; rep from * twice more, ssk, k2tog—35 (37, 41, 49, 53) sts.

Break yarn.

COLLAR

With RS facing, larger needle and MC, starting at right front edge of neck opening, PU and k6 BO sts, PU and k8 (9, 10, 11, 12) sts along side of neck, k 35 (37, 41, 49, 53) sts of fronts, sleeves, and back, PU and k 9 (10, 11, 12, 13) sts along side of neck, PU and k6 BO sts—64 (68, 74, 84, 90) sts.

Row 1 Sl 1 kwise, k1, *k1, p1; rep from * to last 2 sts, k2.

Rep row 1 for 14 rows total.

Break off MC and join CC.

P 1 row, rep row 1.

K 1 row. Break off CC.

Lining

Join lining yarn. With smaller needle, work in St st for 3". Do not BO. Break yarn, leaving a 36" tail.

PATCH

With MC and larger needle, CO 20 sts. Work 32 rows of Patch Chart, then cont in St st with MC until patch measures 14" from beg. BO. Weave in ends.

FINISHING

Sew sleeve seams. Graft underarm sts using kitchener st. Weave in ends. Wash and block sweater and patch.

With CC, baste front edges together. Place zipper on inside of sweater with zipper pull against basted edges. With sewing needle and thread, baste zipper in place. Using a sewing machine or by hand, sew zipper in place. Remove all basting sts.

Fold collar lining under and steam fold flat. Using long tail, sew each live st from last row of lining down to inside of collar. With sewing needle and thread, sew edges of collar lining to back of zipper.

To decide where to place patch, try sweater on with your bag to see where strap falls and wear will occur. This usually necessitates placing the patch up against the beginning of the neck ribbing. Pin patch to shoulder so the skull is at front of sweater. With MC, sew around edge with running st. Weave in ends.

About Adrian I'm a trained artist who's always been obsessed with making stuff. I've studied everything from drawing to painting to glassblowing to metalsmithing, always searching for what felt like my life's work. Little did I know it would turn out to be knitting, which I'd spent my childhood watching my mother and grandmother practice while I took their yarn scraps to make legions of pom-pom animals. I share a wool-filled house in Boston with my husband, Mark, and Shambles, our small terrier, both of whom enjoy a good wool sweater. Visit me on the Web at www.helloyarn.com.

Size

S (M, L, XL, XXL)

Finished chest: 39 (43½, 48, 50, 52)"

Finished length: 26 (27½, 28½, 29½, 31½)"

Materials

MC: Brown Sheep *Lamb's Pride Worsted* (85% wool, 15% mohair; 113g/190 yd), 5 (5, 6, 7, 8) skeins #M-07 Sable

CC: Noro *Kureyon* (100% wool; 50g/109 yd), 3 skeins #164

US 8 (5mm) 16" and 40" circular needles, or size needed to obtain gauge

US 8 (5mm) double-pointed needles (set of 5)

Stitch markers

Waste yarn

Gauge

14 sts and 20 rows = 4" in St st

STEF PULFORD

Hacky Sack Hoodie

If nothing else interests him in a yarn store, a guy will still want to check out the Kureyon, where ten-odd saturated colors coexist on a single skein. This sweater is a great way to knit those self-striping colors into a garment without overpowering it. If you select your yarn cleverly, the stripes will appear to blend out of the main color just as they fade into each other on the skein. For the gentleman who prefers a sportier look, knit the hoodie with a solid stripe or no stripe at all. The top-down raglan requires very little finishing, and it's easy to alter the length—just knit more or fewer rows before the ribbing. Guys like the Hacky Sack because it fits like a refined sweatshirt. But don't keep this one a secret; it'll be more fun to pick out the Kureyon together.

Directions

Note: In order to preserve the subtle fade from the MC yarn to the CC yarn, wind the CC yarn into a center-pull ball until you reach a stretch of a color that's similar to the MC yarn. Cut the CC ball in the center of that stripe. Set the center-pull ball aside and knit with the remaining yarn on the skein until you reach the end, so that there is little contrast between the MC yarn and the CC yarn at the join. Then knit from the center of the ball you wound until you reach the end, which will be a color that's similar to the MC yarn.

HOOD

With 40" needle and MC, CO 31 (31, 32, 32, 32) sts, pm, CO 31 (31, 32, 32, 32) sts—62 (62, 64, 64, 64) sts.

P 1 row.

Inc row (RS) K to 2 sts from marker, kfb, k1, sm, k1, kfb, k to end—64 (64, 66, 66, 66) sts.

Cont in St st, work inc row every RS row 11 (13, 14, 14, 14) times more—86 (90, 94, 94, 94) sts. Work even until hood meas 6 (6½, 8, 9½, 10½)" from beg, ending with a WS row.

Dec row (RS) K to 3 sts from marker, k2tog, k1, sm, k1, k2tog, k to end.

Rep dec row every 4th row 8 (8, 6, 4, 2) times more—68 (72, 80, 84, 88) sts.

Next row (WS) P10 (11, 13, 14, 15) left front sts, pm; p12 left sleeve sts, pm (end of rnd); p24 (26, 30, 32, 34) back sts removing hood marker, pm; p12 right sleeve sts, pm; p10 (11, 13, 14, 15) right front sts.

BODY

Neck

Row 1 (RS) K1, kfb, *k to 1 st from marker, kfb, sm, kfb; rep from * 3 times more, k to last 3 sts, kfb, k2—10 sts increased.

Row 2 P2, pfb, p to last 2 sts, pfb, p1.

Rep last 2 rows 2 (2, 3, 3, 4) times more—104 (108, 128, 132, 148) sts.

Rep row 1 once more, omitting first and last kfb, and ending 8 (8, 12, 12, 16) sts from end of row.

Sl first 8 (8, 12, 12, 16) sts of last row onto a dpn and place in front of sts at end of row.

Join round creating overlap by *knitting next st on dpn tog with next st on circular needle; rep from * until all

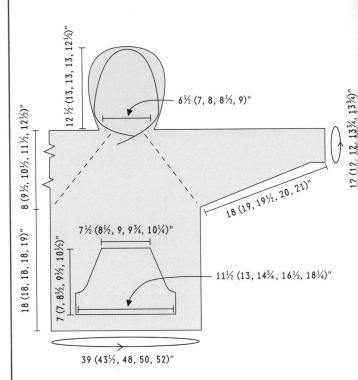

12½ (13, 13, 13, 12½)"

6½ (7, 8, 8½, 9)"

12 (12, 12, 13¾, 13¾)"

8 (9½, 10½, 11½, 12½)"

18 (19, 19½, 20, 21)"

7½ (8½, 9, 9¾, 10¼)"

18 (18, 18, 18, 19)"

7 (7, 8½, 9½, 10½)"

11½ (13, 14¾, 16½, 18¼)"

39 (43½, 48, 50, 52)"

8 (8, 12, 12, 16) sts on dpn have been worked, k to end of rnd—104 (108, 124, 128, 140) sts. K 1 rnd.

Raglan Shaping

Inc rnd *Kfb, k to 1 st from marker, kfb, sm; rep from * 3 times more.

Rep inc rnd every other rnd 15 (18, 20, 23, 24) times more, changing to longer needle when necessary—232 (260, 284, 312, 340) sts: 64 (72, 80, 88, 92) sts each front and back; 52 (58, 62, 68, 70) sts each sleeve.

Place each set of sleeve sts on wy.

Remove beg of rnd marker, CO 2 (2, 2, 0, 0) sts, pm for new beg of rnd, CO 2 (2, 2, 0, 0) more sts, rm, k to next marker, rm, CO 2 (2, 2, 0, 0) sts, pm, CO 2 (2, 2, 0, 0) more sts, rm—136 (152, 168, 176, 184) sts. K 5 (6, 7, 7, 7) rnds.

Break off MC, and join CC (shifting colors as noted). Work even in St st for 1 skein CC. Join MC and cont in St st until body meas 16 (17, 17, 17, 18)" from first raglan inc.

Pocket

Next rnd K21 (23, 26, 27, 28) front sts, then with short needle k26 (30, 32, 34, 36). Leave rem body sts on long circular and work pocket back and forth on short circular needle.

Cont in St st, inc every 4th row 5 (5, 6, 6, 7) times, then every other row 2 (3, 4, 6, 7) times as foll: K1, kfb, k to last 3 sts, kfb, k2—40 (46, 52, 58, 64) sts after all inc. (*Note:* This sounds like it'll create mismatched areas at the pocket edge, but you'll find that offsetting the kfb increases makes the pocket look more symmetric.)

Work even in St st for 10 rows. Place sts on wy. Break yarn.

Return to body sts and rejoin MC. PU and k26 (30, 32, 34, 36) sts across WS of first row of pocket, k to end of rnd. K 34 (36, 42, 46, 52) rnds to match pocket length.

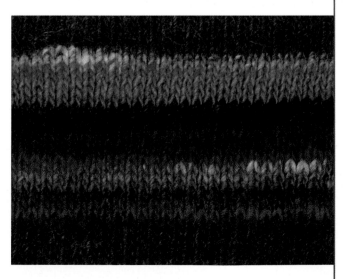

Joining rnd K14 (15, 16, 15, 14), join pocket to body by *knitting 1 st from pocket together with 1 st from body; rep from * until all pocket sts are worked, k to end of rnd.

Ribbing

Next rnd Inc 2 (1, 0, 1, 2) sts evenly around—138 (153, 168, 177, 186) sts.

Work in k2, p1 rib for 14 rows. BO loosely in rib.

SLEEVES (MAKE 2)

Place 52 (58, 62, 68, 70) sleeve sts onto short circular needle. Join MC and k to underarm, PU and k2 (2, 2, 0, 0) sts from body underarm, pm for beg of rnd, PU and k2 (2, 2, 0, 0) sts, k to end—56 (62, 66, 68, 70) sts. K 2 rnds. Break off MC and join CC (shifting colors as noted). K 3 rnds.

Dec rnd K2tog, k to last 2 sts, ssk.

Cont in St st, rep dec rnd every 6th rnd 6 (9, 11, 9, 10) times more, changing to dpns when necessary. When CC skein is finished, join MC and cont in St st for rem of dec—42 (42, 42, 48, 48) sts.

Work even in St st until sleeve meas 15 (16, 16½, 17, 18)".

Work in k2, p1 rib for 14 rnds. BO loosely in rib.

FINISHING

Weave in ends. With MC and tapestry needle, sew side edges of last 10 rows of pocket to body. Sew seam at top of hood, starting at first and last sts of CO row.

About Stef As a young DIY savant, I wanted to learn every needlecraft in existence. This quest ended prematurely around the time when I realized I had no particular use for tatting. I like useful things, you see, which is probably why I've stuck with knitting for twenty years. It's also why I became an engineer. I live in Davis, CA, where I make the best baklava around. I do not blog about useful things or baklava at www.knitthehellup.com.

ANDREW STEINBRECHER

Ernie Sweater

Boys will be boys, even if they're men, and this sweater will help any guy get in touch with his inner child. I originally designed this project in a different color scheme, but I always called it my "Ernie" sweater and finally decided to take that thought to its brightly colored conclusion. Immediately recognizable as the outfit of everyone's favorite muppet, this playful project is done in incredibly soft, sproingy merino yarn that will baby any man. It's so fun to make, it may even have you singing "Ernie Sweater, you're the one, You make knitting lots of fun. Ernie Sweater, I'm awfully fond of you."

Stripe pattern

8 rows A, 2 rows D, 8 rows B, 2 rows C.

Directions

BACK

With smaller needles and C, CO 94 (102, 110, 122, 130) sts.

Row 1 (RS) K2, *p2, k2; rep from * to end.

Row 2 P2, *k2, p2; rep from * to end.

Rows 3–10 Rep rows 1 and 2, inc 0 (0, 2, 0, 0) sts on last row.

Change to larger needles. Break off C and join A.

Work in St st in Stripe patt until back meas approx 16 (16, 16, 18, 18)" from beg, ending with a D (D, D, C, C) stripe.

BO 5 (7, 9, 12, 14) sts at beg of next 2 rows—84 (88, 94, 98, 102) sts.

Size

S (M, L, XL, XXL)

Finished chest: 40 (44, 48, 52, 56)"

Finished length: 24½ (25, 25½, 28, 28½)"

Materials

Karabella *Aurora 8* (100% wool; 50g/98 yd)

A: 5 (5, 6, 7, 8) balls #7 vermillion

B: 5 (5, 6, 7, 8) balls #15 royal blue

C: 3 (3, 4, 4, 5) balls #36 yellow

D: 2 (2, 3, 3, 3) balls #1250 white

US 7 (4.5mm) straight needles and 16" circular needle

US 9 (5.5mm) straight needles, or size needed to obtain gauge

Gauge

18½ sts and 25 rows = 4" in St st using larger needles

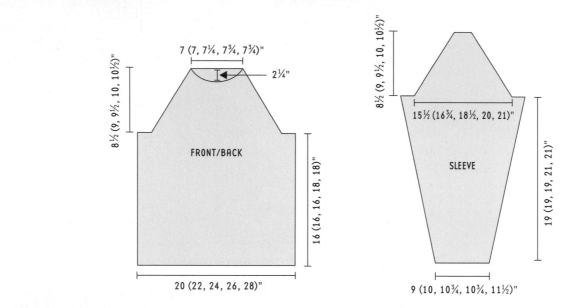

7 (7, 7¼, 7¾, 7¾)"

2¼"

8½ (9, 9½, 10, 10½)"

FRONT/BACK

16 (16, 16, 18, 18)"

20 (22, 24, 26, 28)"

8½ (9, 9½, 10, 10½)"

15½ (16¾, 18½, 20, 21)"

SLEEVE

19 (19, 19, 21, 21)"

9 (10, 10¾, 10¾, 11½)"

Raglan Shaping

Row 1 (RS) K2, skp, k to last 4 sts, k2tog, k2.

Row 2 Purl.

Rep rows 1 and 2 until 32 (32, 34, 36, 36) sts rem.

BO loosely.

FRONT

Work same as back until 46 (46, 48, 50, 50) sts rem, ending with a WS row.

Neck Shaping

Row 1 (RS) K2, skp, k10, join 2nd ball of yarn and BO next 18 (18, 20, 22, 22) sts, k to last 4 sts, k2tog, k2.

Row 2 and all even rows Working both sides at once, purl.

Rows 3, 5, 7 *K2, skp, k to last 4 sts, k2tog, k2; rep from * on other side.

Row 9 *K1, skp, k1, k2tog, k1; rep from * on other side—5 sts.

Row 11 *K1, sk2p, k1; rep from * on other side—3 sts.

Row 13 *Sk2p; rep from * on other side—1 st.

Fasten off.

SLEEVES (MAKE 2)

With smaller needles and C, CO 42 (46, 46, 50, 54) sts.

Work in k2, p2 rib same as back for 10 rows total.

Change to larger needles. Break off C and join B.

Inc row (RS) K1, kfb, k to last 2 sts, kfb, k1.

Cont in St st in Stripe patt, rep inc row every 4th row 0 (0, 5, 4, 7) times, then every 6th row 14 (15, 14, 16, 14) times—72 (78, 86, 92, 98) sts. Cont even in Stripe patt until sleeve meas 19 (19, 19, 21, 21)" from beg, ending with a D (D, D, C, C) stripe.

BO 5 (7, 9, 12, 14) sts at beg of next 2 rows—62 (64, 68, 68, 70) sts.

Work raglan shaping same as back until 10 (8, 8, 6, 4) sts rem.

BO loosely.

FINISHING

Block pieces to measurements. With RS facing, sew raglan, side and sleeve seams.

Neckband

With RS facing, smaller needle and C, starting at left back shoulder seam, PU and k92 sts evenly around neck opening. Pm and work in k2, p2 rib for 8 rnds. BO loosely in rib.

Weave in ends. Put on sweater and grab your rubber ducky.

About Andrew I'm a graphic designer and live in Cincinnati. I started knitting four years ago to control anxiety, and I've knit constantly ever since. When I'm not knitting, I can be found teaching competitive color guard at one of those big suburban high schools or swooning over mid-century modern furniture. My ultimate dream is to learn French and move to Paris. Watch my life at www.drew-o-rama.com.

Size

S (M, L, XL, XXL)

Finished chest: 38 (44, 46, 50, 54)"

Finished length: 24 (25½, 26¾, 27½, 28¼)"

Materials

Rowan *Cashsoft Aran* (57% merino wool, 33% microfiber, 10% cashmere; 50g/95 yd)

MC: 9 (10, 11, 13, 14) skeins #03 Mole

CC1: 3 (3, 4, 4, 4) skeins #01 Oat

CC2: 2 (2, 2, 3, 3) skeins #04 Haze

US 6 (4mm) 40" circular needle

US 7 (4.5mm) 40" circular needle, or size needed to obtain gauge

Five 1" diameter buttons

Stitch holders or waste yarn

Stitch markers

Sewing needle and matching thread

Gauge

19 sts and 26 rows = 4" in St st using larger needle

JENNIFER COHEN

Retropolitan Cardigan

I was inspired to design this sweater after coming across a picture of my parents from the '70s in which my dad was wearing a baby blue cardigan. It was a classic design befitting the disco decade when worn with a button-down-collar shirt. I updated the design by using longer ribbing, bold stripes, and oversized buttons. The color combination of light blue, cream, and taupe was inspired by a pair of men's argyle-patterned sneakers I bought when the shoe store ran out of the pink version for women. I guess everything does happen for a reason! The beauty of the Retropolitan Cardigan is that it can be worn by trendy urbanites, indie rockers, and computer nerds alike. A traditional man may prefer the sweater in a solid color and paired with a shirt and tie, while a more fashion-forward guy might like the stripes in offbeat colors and worn over his favorite band's T-shirt.

Stripe pattern

*4 rows MC, 1 row CC1, 1 row CC2, 4 rows MC, 2 rows CC1, 1 row CC2, 1 row MC, 1 row CC2, 2 rows CC1, 4 rows MC, 1 row CC2, 1 row CC1; rep from *.

Directions

Note: The body is knit in one piece from the bottom up to the armholes. Then the sleeves are knit flat, the sleeve seams are sewn, the sleeves are attached,

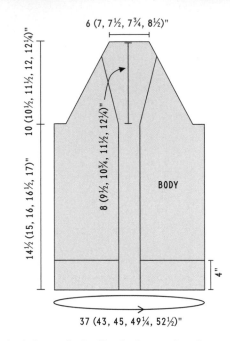

6 (7, 7½, 7¾, 8½)"

10 (10½, 11½, 12, 12¼)"

8 (9½, 10¾, 11½, 12¼)"

14½ (15, 16, 16½, 17)"

BODY

4"

37 (43, 45, 49¼, 52½)"

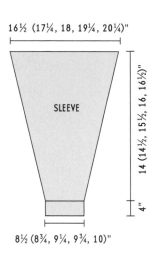

16½ (17¼, 18, 19¼, 20¼)"

SLEEVE

14 (14½, 15½, 16, 16½)"

4"

8½ (8¾, 9¼, 9¾, 10)"

and the raglan yoke is formed. Finally, the button band is picked up and worked around the perimeter and the buttons are sewn on.

BODY

With smaller needle and MC, CO 160 (188, 196, 212, 228) sts. Work 23 rows in k2, p2 rib as foll: K1, p2, *k2, p2; rep from * to last st, k1.

Cont in k2, p2 rib as est, beg Stripe patt, inc 16 (16, 18, 22, 22) sts evenly around on first row—176 (204, 214, 234, 250) sts. Change to larger needle. Cont even in St st Stripe patt until body meas 14½ (15, 16, 16½, 17)" from beg, ending with a WS row. Place sts on holder or wy and set aside.

SLEEVES (MAKE 2)

With smaller needle and MC, CO 40 (42, 44, 46, 48) sts.

Row 1 (WS) P1 (2, 1, 2, 1), k2, *p2, k2; rep from * to last 1 (2, 1, 2, 1) sts, p to end.

Row 2 K1 (2, 1, 2, 1), *p2, k2; rep from * to last

3 (4, 3, 4, 3) sts, p2, k to end.

Work a total of 26 rows k2, p2 rib as est.

Beg St st Stripe patt, inc 6 (6, 6, 8, 8) sts evenly across first row—46 (48, 50, 54, 56) sts.

Change to larger needle. Cont in patt, inc 1 st each side every 4th row 4 (4, 4, 4, 5) times, then every 6th row 12 (13, 14, 15, 15) times—78 (82, 86, 92, 96) sts.

Cont even in patt until sleeve meas 18 (18½, 19½, 20, 20½)" from beg, ending with a WS row and at the same place in stripe sequence as body.

Place first and last 8 (8, 8, 9, 9) sts onto wy. Cut all yarns, leaving 8" tails.

Sew sleeve seam, taking care to match all stripes.

JOIN SLEEVES TO BODY

Cont in patt on body, k37 (44, 46, 50, 54), pm, place next 14 (14, 14, 16, 16) body sts on wy for underarm; cont in body patt as est, k62 (66, 70, 74, 78) sleeve sts, pm; k74 (88,

94, 102, 110) body sts, pm; place next 14 (14, 14, 16, 16) sts on wy for underarm; k62 (66, 70, 74, 78) sleeve sts, pm; k37 (44, 46, 50, 54) body sts—272 (308, 326, 350, 374) sts.

Raglan Shaping

Work even in patt for 7 (3, 5, 1, 1) rows.

Dec row (RS) *K to 4 sts from marker, ssk, k2, sm, k2, k2tog; rep from * 3 times more, k to end of row.

Rep dec row every RS row 23 (26, 28, 32, 33) times more, then every 4th row 3 times.

AT THE SAME TIME, when piece meas 16" from beg, shape neck by dec 1 st each end of next row and every foll 4th row 8 (12, 12, 12, 15) times total, then every 6th row twice.

When piece meas 24 (25½, 26¾, 27½, 28¼)" and raglan shaping is complete, BO.

FINISHING

Graft underarm sts, picking up extra sts at each side of underarm sts to prevent gaps.

Button Band

With RS facing, smaller needle and MC, and starting at lower right edge, PU and k76 sts to beg of neck shaping, pm, 37 (45, 50, 54, 57) sts along right front neck, 8 (6, 6, 2, 4) sleeve sts, 20 (28, 30, 30, 36) sts across back neck, 8 (6, 6, 2, 4) sleeve sts, 37 (45, 50, 54, 57) sts along left front neck, pm, 76 sts to lower left edge—262 (282, 294, 294, 310) sts.

Work in k2, p2 rib for 3 rows, beg with p2 on first row. Mark placement for 5 buttonholes.

Buttonhole row *Rib to 1 st before marked st, BO 3 sts; rep from * 4 times more, rib to end.

Next row *Rib to BO sts of previous row, CO 3 sts; rep from * 4 times more, rib to end.

Cont in rib for 4 more rows. BO in rib.

Using sewing needle and thread, sew buttons opposite buttonholes.

About Jennifer I learned to knit and crochet at the tender age of twelve from an after-school program supplemented by my grandmother's patience. When I moved to New York City years later, I made it home by exploring the LYSs in each neighborhood and starting my own SnB: the Upper East Side Knitters. When not trying to obtain gauge, I love to travel (especially if a sheep and wool festival is involved), am an avid theater-goer, and recently started making my own jewelry and clay beads. I fund my addiction through employment as a registered dietitian and am working on somehow combining knitting and nutrition— knutrition anyone? Read all about it on my blog: knittingknews.blogspot.com.

DEBBIE STOLLER

Checks & Balances

This snuggly pullover was inspired by my brother's favorite sweater. Done up in taxi-cab yellow, in gorgeous merino wool from a small producer in upstate New York, this sweater is simple to knit and has a subtle overall checkered pattern that's incredibly versatile: He can throw on a leather biker jacket and hit the road, pair it with pinstripe pants for a hip night out at the pool hall, or wear it with jeans for a hike in the woods. Or, if made in a smoother yarn and a more neutral shade such as khaki or gray, it can even look quite businesslike. (Just be sure to keep the color light, or you won't be able to see the fun stitching.) However he wears it, this one's guaranteed to keep him warm and comfy all day long.

Size

S (M, L, XL, XXL)

Finished chest: 40 (44, 48, 52, 56)"

Finished length: 25 (26, 26½, 27½, 28)"

Materials

Morehouse Merino 3-Strand (100% merino wool; 2oz/140 yd), 8 (9, 9, 10, 10) skeins Sunflower

US 7 (4.5mm) straight needles, or size needed to obtain gauge

US 7 (4.5mm) 16" circular needle

Stitch holder

Gauge

16 sts and 24 rows = 4" in St st

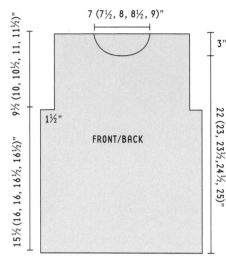

7 (7½, 8, 8½, 9)"

9½ (10, 10½, 11, 11½)"

3"

1½"

FRONT/BACK

22 (23, 23½, 24½, 25)"

15½ (16, 16, 16½, 16½)"

20½ (22½, 24½, 26½, 28½)"

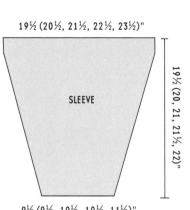

19½ (20½, 21½, 22½, 23½)"

SLEEVE

19½ (20, 21, 21½, 22)"

9½ (9½, 10½, 10½, 11½)"

Directions

BACK

With straight needles, CO 82 (90, 98, 106, 114) sts.

Row 1 *K2, p2; rep from * to last 2 sts, k2.

Row 2 *P2, k2; rep from * to last 2 sts, p2.

Rep rows 1 and 2 until piece meas 2" from beg, ending with a WS row.

Begin check patt as foll:

Row 1 (RS) K6 (3, 0, 4, 1), *k6, p1, k7; rep from * to last 6 (3, 0, 4, 1) sts, p6 (3, 0, 4, 1).

Row 2 P6 (3, 0, 4, 1) *p6, k1, p7; rep from * to last 6 (3, 0, 4, 1) sts, k6 (3, 0, 4, 1).

Rows 3–16 Rep rows 1 and 2.

Row 17 Rep row 1.

Row 18 (WS) Knit.

Rep rows 1–18 until piece meas 15½ (16, 16, 16½, 16½)" from beg, ending with a WS row. Maintaining patt

as est, BO 6 sts at beg of next 2 rows—70 (78, 86, 94, 102) sts.

Continue in patt until piece meas 25 (26, 26½, 27½, 28)" from beg. BO 21 (24, 27, 30, 33) sts, work across center 28 (30, 32, 34, 36) sts, BO rem 21 (24, 27, 30, 33) sts. Place center sts on holder for back neck.

FRONT

Work same as for back until piece meas 22 (23, 23½, 24½, 25)" from beg, ending with a WS row. Maintaining patt as est, work 32 (36, 39, 42, 45) sts, join a 2nd ball of yarn and BO next 6 (6, 8, 10, 12) sts, work rem 32 (36, 39, 42, 45) sts. Working both sides at the same time, BO 3 (4, 4, 4, 4) sts at neck edge once; 2 sts twice; and 1 st every other row 4 times. Work even in patt as est until front matches back. BO rem 21 (24, 27, 30, 33) sts each shoulder.

SLEEVES (MAKE 2)

CO 38 (38, 42, 46, 46) sts.

Row 1 (RS) *K2, p2; rep from * to last 2 sts, k2.

Row 2 *P2, k2; rep from * to last 2 sts, p2.

Rep rows 1 and 2 until piece meas 2" from beg, ending with a WS row.

Begin check patt as foll:

Row 1 K5 (5, 0, 2, 2), *k6, p1, k7; rep from * to last 5 (5, 0, 2, 2) sts, k5 (5, 0, 2, 2).

Row 2 P5 (5, 0, 2, 2), *p6, k1, p7; rep from * to last 5 (5, 0, 2, 2) sts, p5 (5, 0, 2, 2).

Rows 3–16 Rep rows 1 and 2.

Row 17 Rep row 1.

Row 18 Knit.

Rep rows 1–18. AT SAME TIME, maintaining patt as est, inc 1 st each side every 4th row 14 (18, 15, 13, 18) times, then every 6th row 6 (4, 7, 9, 6) times—78 (82, 86, 90, 94) sts.

Cont even in patt as est until piece meas 19½ (20, 21, 21½, 22)" from beg.

BO all sts.

FINISHING

Sew shoulder seams, matching pattern sts on front and back pieces. Place 28 (30, 32, 34, 36) back neck sts on circular needle, then PU and k32 (34, 36, 38, 40) sts evenly around front neck—60 (64, 68, 72, 76) sts. Work in k2, p2 rib for 2".

BO very loosely in rib. Sew sleeves into armholes, matching center of sleeve to shoulder seam. Sew sleeve and side seams. Weave in ends. Block gently.

Size

S (M, L, XL, XXL)

Finished chest: 41 (45, 49, 52, 56)"

Finished length: 24½ (25½, 26½, 27½, 28½)"

Materials

Rowan Classic *Cashsoft DK* (57% extra-fine merino, 33% microfiber, 10% cashmere; 50g/142 yd), 16 (17, 19, 21, 21) skeins #523 Lichen

G/6 (4mm) and F/5 (3.75mm) crochet hooks, or sizes required to obtain gauge

Gauge

9 sts = 2" and 8 rows =2½" in pattern

PETER FRANZI

Gatsby

This sweater design is the result of years of frustration with not finding suitable, wearable, and fashionable crocheted garments for men. I've always been fascinated with texture, and this project's got plenty. While the pattern may seem daunting, the main sequence is mastered with a little determination, and there is enough variety in stitches to keep you engaged in your work. Made in a soft cashmere blend, it drapes so nicely that no one would guess it was crocheted. The Gatsby sweater is especially smart in earthy, solid tones. It's a classic design that will look equally at home at a Hamptons garden party (while you're sipping a martini, of course) or at the local dive bar where you're downing a PBR.

Double Crochet Decrease (DD)

Yo, insert hook in next st, yo and pull up a lp, yo and pull through 2 lps (2 lps now on hook), yo, insert hook in next st, yo and pull up a lp, yo and pull through 2 lps, yo and pull through 3 lps.

Modified Half Double Crochet Decrease (MHDD)

Yo, insert hook in first st, yo and pull up a lp, insert hook in next st, yo and pull up a lp, yo and pull through 4 lps.

Front Post Double Crochet (FPdc)

Yo, insert hook from front to back to front around post of indicated stitch, yo and pull up a lp, (yo and pull through 2 lps) twice.

Back Post Double Crochet (BPdc)

Yo, insert hook from back to front to back around post of indicated stitch, yo and pull up a lp, (yo and pull through 2 lps) twice.

Pattern sequences

Patt A: Sk next st, dc in next st; working in front of last dc made, dc in skipped st

Patt B: Sk next st, dc in next st; working behind last dc made, dc in skipped st

Directions

Note: Do not skip the first stitch (**DNS1S**) in the row throughout as indicated. The beginning ch and the following dec st are the first two sts of the row (2 sts but 3 posts). Likewise, at the ends of the rows the dec st plus the final dc (or hdc) render 2 sts but 3 posts. This unusual sequence is used to eliminate the "hole" between the beg ch and the first st.

BACK

With larger hook, ch 94 (102, 110, 118, 126).

Row 1 Sc in 2nd ch from hook and in each ch across—93 (101, 109, 117, 125) sc. Turn.

Row 2 (RS) Ch 3, (DNS1S), DD, work patt A 8 (9, 10, 11, 12) times, FPdc in next 2 sts, [dc in next st, FPdc in next 2 sts] twice, work patt A 7 (8, 9, 10, 11) times, FPdc in next st, dc in next st, FPdc in next 2 sts, dc in next st, FPdc in next 3 sts, dc in next st, FPdc in next 2 sts, dc in next st, FPdc in next st, work patt A 7 (8, 9, 10, 11) times, FPdc in next 2 sts, [dc in next st, FPdc in next 2 sts]

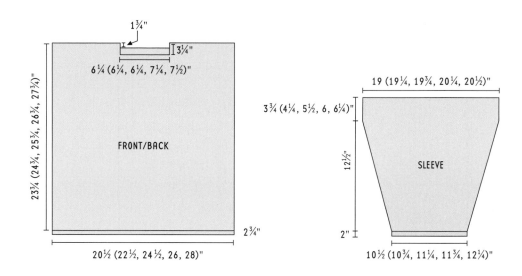

twice, work patt A 8 (9, 10, 11, 12) times, DD, dc in same st (last st used in DD)—93 (101, 109, 117, 125) sts. Turn.

Row 3 Ch 2, (DNS1S), MHDD, hdc in next 16 (18, 20, 22, 24) sts, BPdc in next 2 sts, [hdc in next st, BPdc in next 2 sts] twice, hdc in next 14 (16, 18, 20, 22) sts, BPdc in next st, hdc in next dc, BPdc in next 2 sts, hdc in next dc, BPdc in next 3 sts, hdc in next st, BPdc in next 2 sts, hdc in next st, BPdc in next st, hdc in next 14 (16, 18, 20, 22) sts, BPdc in next 2 sts, [hdc in next st, BPdc in next 2 sts] twice, hdc in next 16 (18, 20, 22, 24) sts, MHDD, hdc in same st (last st used in MHDD)—93 (101, 109, 117, 125) sts. Turn.

Row 4 Ch 3, (DNS1S), DD, work patt B 8 (9, 10, 11, 12) times, FPdc in next 2 sts, [dc in next st, FPdc in next 2 sts] twice, work patt B 7 (8, 9, 10, 11) times, FPdc in next st, dc in next st, FPdc in next 2 sts, dc in next st, FPdc in next 3 sts, dc in next st, FPdc in next 2 sts, dc in next st, FPdc in next st, work patt B 7 (8, 9, 10, 11) times, FPdc in next 2 sts, [dc in next st, FPdc in next 2 sts] twice,

work patt B 8 (9, 10, 11, 12) times, DD, dc in same st (last st used in DD)—93 (101, 109, 117, 125) sts.

Row 5 Rep row 3.

Rep rows 2–5 until front meas approx 22 (23, 24, 25, 26)", ending with a WS row. Do not fasten off.

Shape Right Neck

Row 1 (RS) Ch 3, (DNS1S), DD, work patt B or A 8 (9 ,10, 11, 12) times, FPdc in next 2 sts, [dc in next st, FPdc in next 2 sts] twice, work patt B or A 2 (3, 4, 4, 5) times, DD, dc in last st used in DD—32 (36, 40, 42, 46) sts. Turn, leaving rem sts unworked.

Row 2 Ch 2, (DNS1S), MHDD, hdc in next 4 (6, 8, 8, 10) sts, BPdc in next 2 sts, [hdc in next st, BPdc in next 2 sts] twice, hdc in next 16 (18, 20, 22, 24) sts, MHDD, hdc in last st used in MHDD.

Rows 3–6 Rep rows 1 and 2.

Fasten off.

Shape Left Neck

With RS facing, sk next 29 (29, 29, 33, 33) sts. Join yarn in next st.

Row 1 Ch 3, DD in same st and in next st, work patt B or A 2 (3, 4, 4, 5) times, FPdc in next 2 sts, [dc in next st, FPdc in next 2 sts] twice, work patt B or A 8 (9, 10, 11, 12) times, DD, dc in last st used in DD—32 (36, 40, 42, 46) sts. Turn.

Row 2 Ch 2, (DNS1S), MHDD, hdc in next 16 (18, 20, 22, 24) sts, BPdc in next 2 sts, [hdc in next st, BPdc in next 2 sts] twice, hdc in next 4 (6, 8, 8, 10) sts, MHDD, hdc in last st used in MHDD.

Row 3 Ch 3, (DNS1S), DD, work patt A or B 2 (3, 4, 4, 5) times, FPdc in next 2 sts, [dc in next st, FPdc in next 2 sts] twice, work patt A or B 8 (9, 10, 11, 12) times, DD, dc in last st used in DD.

Row 4 Rep row 2.

Row 5 Ch 3, (DNS1S), DD, work patt B or A 2 (3, 4, 4, 5) times, FPdc in next 2 sts, [dc in next st, FPdc in next 2 sts] twice, work patt B or A 8 (9, 10, 11, 12) times, DD, dc in last st used in DD—32 (36, 40, 42, 46) sts. Turn.

Row 6 Rep row 2.

Fasten off.

FRONT

Work same as back until front meas 20½ (21½, 22½, 23½, 24½)", ending with a WS row. Do not fasten off.

Shape Left Neck

Rows 1–5 Same as back right neck.

Rows 6–9 Rep rows 2–5.

Rows 10–11 Rep rows 2–3.

Fasten off.

Shape Right Neck

Rows 1–5 Same as back left neck.

Rows 6–9 Rep rows 2–5.

Rows 10–11 Rep rows 2–3.

Fasten off.

RIBBING (MAKE 2)

With smaller hook, ch 16.

Row 1 Sc in 2nd ch from hook and in each ch across—15 sc. Turn.

Row 2 Ch 1, working through back lps only, sc in each sc across. Turn.

Rows 3–93 (101, 109, 117, 125) Rep row 2. Do not turn after last row.

Edging row Ch 1, rotate and work 1 sc in end of each row along length of ribbing—93 (101, 109, 117, 125) sc.

Fasten off.

With RS facing, attach ribbing to lower edge of back, working through both lps of edging row. Rep for front.

SLEEVES (MAKE 2)

With larger hook, ch 48 (50, 52, 54, 56).

Row 1 Sc in 2nd ch from hook and in each ch across—47 (49, 51, 53, 55) sc. Turn.

Row 2 (RS) Ch 3, (DNS1S), DD, work patt A 8 (8, 8, 9, 9) times, FPdc in next 1 (1, 2, 1, 2) sts, dc in next st, FPdc in next 1 (2, 2, 2, 2) sts, dc in next st, FPdc in next 3 sts, dc in next st, FPdc in next 1 (2, 2, 2, 2) sts, dc in next st, FPdc in next 1 (1, 2, 1, 2) sts, work patt A 8 (8, 8, 9, 9) times, DD, dc in last st used in DD—47 (49, 51, 53, 55) sts. Turn.

Row 3 (inc) Ch 2, (DNS1S), MHDD, 2 hdc in next st (inc), hdc in next 15 (15, 15, 17, 17) sts, *BPdc in next 1 (1, 2, 1, 2) sts, hdc in next st, BPdc in next 1 (2, 2, 2, 2) sts, hdc in next st, BPdc in next 3 sts, hdc in next st, BPdc in next 1 (2, 2, 2, 2) sts, hdc in next st, BPdc

in next 1 (1, 2, 1, 2) sts*, hdc in next 15 (15, 15, 17, 17) sts, 2 hdc in next st (inc), MHDD, hdc in last st used in MHDD—49 (51, 53, 55, 57) sts. Turn.

Row 4 Ch 3, (DNS1S), DD, dc in next st, work patt B 8 (8, 8, 9, 9) times, FPdc in next 1 (1, 2, 1, 2) sts, dc in next st, FPdc in next 1 (2, 2, 2, 2) sts, dc in next st, FPdc in next 3 sts, dc in next st, FPdc in next 1 (2, 2, 2, 2) sts, dc in next st, FPdc in next 1 (1, 2, 1, 2) sts, work patt B 8 (8, 8, 9, 9) times, dc in next st, DD, dc in last st used in DD. Turn.

Row 5 (inc) Ch 2, (DNS1S), MHDD, 2 hdc in next st (inc), hdc in next 16 (16, 16, 18, 18) sts, work from * to * of row 3, hdc in next 16 (16, 16, 18, 18) sts, 2 hdc in next st (inc), work MHDD, hdc in last st used in MHDD—51 (53, 55, 57, 59) sts. Turn.

Row 6 Ch 3, (DNS1S), DD, work patt A 9 (9, 9, 10, 10) times, FPdc in next 1 (1, 2, 1, 2) sts, dc in next st, FPdc in next 1 (2, 2, 2, 2) sts, dc in next st, FPdc in next 3 sts, dc in next st, FPdc in next 1 (2, 2, 2, 2) sts, dc in next st, FPdc in next 1 (1, 2, 1, 2) sts, work patt A 9 (9, 9, 10, 10) times, DD, dc in last st used in DD. Turn.

Rows 7–38 Rep rows 3–6, inc 2 sts every WS row and working inc sts into patt as est—83 (85, 87, 89, 91) sts after row 38.

Row 39 (inc) Inc once more each side, keeping in patts as est—85 (87, 89, 91, 93) sts.

Row 40 Ch 3, (DNS1S), DD, dc in next st, work patt B 17 (17, 17, 18, 18) times, *FPdc in next 1 (1, 2, 1, 2) sts, dc in next st, FPdc in next 1 (2, 2, 2, 2) sts, dc in next st, FPdc in next 3 sts, dc in next st, FPdc in next 1 (2, 2, 2, 2) sts, dc in next st, FPdc in next 1 (1, 2, 1, 2) sts, *work patt B 17 (17, 17, 18, 18) times, dc in next st, DD, dc in last st used in DD. Turn.

Row 41 Ch 2, (DNS1S), MHDD, hdc in next 35 (35, 35, 37, 37) sts, BPdc in next 1 (1, 2, 1, 2) sts, hdc in next st, BPdc in next 1 (2, 2, 2, 2) sts, hdc in next st, BPdc in next 3 sts, hdc in next st, BPdc in next 1 (2, 2, 2, 2) sts, hdc in next st, BPdc in next 1 (1, 2, 1, 2) sts, hdc in next 35 (35, 35, 37, 37) sts, MHDD, hdc in last st used in MHDD. Turn.

Row 42 Ch 3, (DNS1S), DD, dc in next st, work patt A 17 (17, 17, 18, 18) times, work from * to * of row 40, work patt A 17 (17, 17, 18, 18) times, dc in next st, DD, dc in last st used in DD. Turn.

Row 43 Rep row 41.

Row 44 Rep row 40.

Rows 45–52 Rep rows 41–44 twice.

Size S only: Fasten off.

Rows 53–54 Rep rows 41–42.

Size M only: Fasten off.

Rows 55–56 Rep rows 43–44.

Row 57 Rep row 43.

Size L only: Fasten off.

Rows 58–59 Rep rows 42–43.

Size XL only: Fasten off.

Row 60 Rep row 44.

Size XXL only: Fasten off.

CUFF (MAKE 2)

With smaller hook, ch 12.

Row 1 Sc in 2nd ch from hook and in each ch across—11 sc. Turn.

Row 2 Ch 1, working through back lps only, sc in each sc across—11 sc. Turn.

Rows 3–47 (49, 51, 53, 55) Rep row 2.

Edging row Ch 1, rotate and work 1 sc in end of each row along length of cuff—47 (49, 51, 53, 55) sc.

Fasten off.

With RS facing, attach cuff to lower edge of sleeve, working through both lps of edging row.

COLLAR

With smaller hook, ch 22.

Row 1 Sc in 2nd ch from hook and in each ch across—21 sc. Turn.

Row 2 Ch 1, working through back lps only, sc in each sc across—21 sc. Turn.

Rows 3–106 (106, 106, 114, 114) Rep row 2.

Edging row Ch 1, rotate and work 1 sc in end of each row along length of collar—106 (106, 106, 114, 114) sc.

Fasten off.

FINISHING

With RS tog, join front to back at shoulders. With RS tog, attach sleeves to body, matching center of sleeve to shoulder seam. Sew sleeve seam, starting at cuff, then continue along side seam to join from underarm to ribbing, taking care to match rows.

Neck

Join yarn to center stitch at back of neck.

Rnd 1 Ch 1, sc in same st, sc in next 14 (14 ,14, 16, 16) sts, sc 24 evenly spaced along side of neck, sc 29 (29, 29, 33, 33) across front neck, sc 24 evenly spaced along other side of neck, sc in rem 14 (14, 14, 16, 16) sts at back neck, join with sl st in first sc—106 (106, 106, 114, 114) sts.

Fasten off.

With RS facing and starting at center back neck, attach collar to neck opening, working through both lps of edging row, to left and to right. Sew collar seam, keeping inside edge smooth.

Weave in ends. Fold collar down.

About Peter I had always wanted to learn to crochet, but when I was a child I couldn't find anyone willing to teach my precocious little self. So, at the young age of fifty, I picked up hook and yarn, downloaded instructions from the Internet, and taught myself. It's been my obsession ever since. I am the owner and moderator of the Yahoo group Men Who Crochet, whose membership from all over the world now approaches 400. When I am not hooking, much of my spare time is spent rehearsing and performing with the San Francisco Gay Men's Chorus.

JOSHUA ECKELS

Speed Racer

I'm a design junkie and I truly believe that there is a lot of power in a thoughtfully placed stripe. From bullet trains and vintage racing cars to those hypnotic center lines on the freeway or the graceful ribbon of a skier's path, a long stripe implies speed and direction and brands a player for sport. This racing stripe sweater allows you to pick his favorite team colors and go. Styled like a vintage ski sweater with a roomier jersey fit and a sleek long stripe from collar to cuff, it's the perfect go-to sweater—whether he's playing a game or just watching one on TV.

Directions

BACK

With smaller needles and MC, CO 80 (86, 95, 104, 110) sts.

Row 1 (WS) K2, *p1, k2; rep from * to end.

Row 2 P2, *k1, p2; rep from * to end.

Rows 3–18 Rep rows 1 and 2.

Row 19 Rep row 1, inc 2 (0, 1, 0, 0) sts evenly across—82 (86, 96, 104, 110) sts.

Change to larger needles.

Row 20 Knit.

Continue in St st until piece meas 14½ (14½, 15, 15¼, 15½)", ending with a WS row.

Size

S (M, L, XL, XXL)

Finished chest: 41 (43, 48, 52, 55)"

Finished length: 21 (22, 23½, 23½, 24)

Materials

Tahki Stacy Charles *Donegal Tweed* (100% wool; 100g/183 yd)

MC: 5 (5, 6, 7, 8) skeins #844 blue

CC: 1 skein #832 red orange

US 9 (5.5mm) straight needles, or size needed to obtain gauge

US 8 (5mm) 16" circular needles

Stitch markers

Stitch holder

Gauge

16 sts and 25 rows = 4" in St st on larger needles

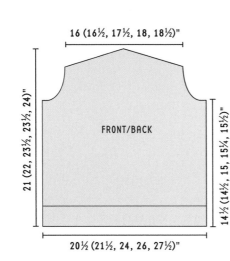

16 (16½, 17½, 18, 18½)"

21 (22, 23½, 23½, 24)"

FRONT/BACK

14½ (14½, 15, 15¼, 15½)"

20½ (21½, 24, 26, 27½)"

15½ (17, 18, 19½, 20½)"

18 (18½, 19, 19½, 20)"

SLEEVE

31 (32½, 33½, 34½, 35½)"

9 (9½, 10½, 11½, 11½)"

Armhole Shaping

BO 3 (3, 5, 6, 6) sts at beg of next 2 rows, then 0 (2, 2, 2, 2) sts at beg of foll 2 rows 0 (1, 2, 2, 3) times—76 (76, 78, 84, 86) sts.

Dec row (RS) K2, ssk, k to last 4 sts, k2tog, k2.

Rep dec row every other row 3 (2, 1, 3, 3) times more, then every 6th row twice—64 (66, 70, 72, 74) sts.

Work even in St st for 5 (9, 9, 7, 5) rows, ending with a WS row.

Short Row Shoulder Shaping

Row 1 K59 (63, 66, 70, 70), W&T; p54 (58, 62, 66, 66), W&T.

Row 2 K49 (54, 58, 62, 62), W&T; p44 (49, 54, 58, 58), W&T.

Row 3 K39 (45, 50, 54, 54), W&T; p34 (41, 46, 50, 50), W&T.

Row 4 K30 (37, 42, 46, 47), W&T; p25 (33, 38, 42, 43), W&T.

Row 5 K21 (29, 34, 38, 40), W&T; p17 (25, 30, 34, 37), W&T.

Row 6 K13 (21, 26, 30, 34), W&T; p9 (17, 22, 26, 31), W&T.

Row 7 K5 (13, 18, 23, 28), W&T; *size S only,* proceed to *; p0 (9, 14, 19, 25), W&T.

Row 8 K0 (5, 11, 16, 22), W&T; *size M only,* proceed to *; p0 (0, 7, 13, 19), W&T.

Row 9 K0 (0, 4, 10, 16), W&T; *size L only,* proceed to *; p0 (0, 0, 7, 13), W&T.

Row 10 K0 (0, 0, 4, 10), W&T; *size XL only,* proceed to *, p0 (0, 0, 0, 7), W&T.

Row 11 K0 (0, 0, 0, 4), W&T; *size XXL,* proceed to *.

*Next row (WS) P1, pm, p to end, PU wraps and p tog with wrapped st.

Next row BO to marker, k to end, PU wraps and k tog with wrapped st.

BO rem sts.

Weave in all ends.

FRONT

Make same as back.

LEFT SLEEVE

With MC and smaller needles, CO 35 (38, 41, 44, 44) sts.

Work in k1, p2 rib for 18 rows as for back.

Row 19 Rep row 1, inc 1 (0, 1, 2, 2) sts evenly across—36 (38, 42, 46, 46) sts.

Row 20 (RS) With MC, k14 (15, 17, 19, 19); join CC and k8; join 2nd ball of MC and k14 (15, 17, 19, 19). *Note:* When changing colors, be sure to twist yarns on WS to prevent holes.

Cont in St st with color stripe as est, work sleeve inc as foll:

Inc row (RS) K2, M1, k to last 2 sts, M1, k2.

Rep inc row every 6th row 7 (14, 12, 14, 15) more times, then every 8th (8th, 8th, 8th, 4th) row 5 (0, 2, 1, 2) times—62 (68, 72, 78, 82) sts.

Work even in St st with color stripe until sleeve meas 18 (18½, 19, 19½, 20)" from beg, ending with a WS row.

Shape Sleeve Cap

BO 3 (3, 4, 5, 3) sts at beg of next 2 rows once (once, once, once, twice).

Dec row (RS) K2, ssk, k to last 4 sts, k2tog, k2.

Rep dec row every other row 1 (2, 2, 2, 2) times more, then every 6th row 2 (2, 2, 3, 3) times—48 (52, 56, 56, 62) sts.

Work even for 3 rows, then rep dec row over next 2 (1, 2, 0, 2) RS rows. P 1 row.

BO 3 (2, 2, 3, 3) sts at beg of next 2 rows, then 0 (3, 2, 3, 3) sts at beg of foll 2 rows—38 (40, 42, 44, 46) sts.

Saddle

Work even in St st with color stripe for 31 (33, 35, 39, 41) rows, ending with a RS row.

Divide for neck opening.

Back Neck

Row 1 (WS) P15 (16, 17, 18, 19) and place these sts on holder for front neck; BO 8 CC sts; p to end—15 (16, 17, 18, 19) sts.

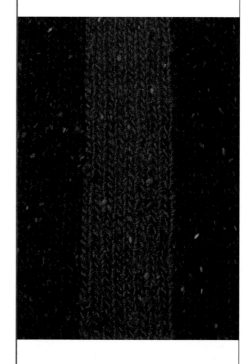

Dec row K to last 3 sts, ssk, k1.

Rep dec row every other row 2 (2, 2, 3, 3) times more; every 4th row 2 (3, 3, 1, 4) times; then every 6th row 1 (1, 1, 2, 0) times—9 (9, 10, 11, 11) sts. Work even for 3 (1, 1, 1, 1) rows. AT THE SAME TIME, starting with row 20 (22, 22, 22, 22), BO 3 sts at beg of next 2 RS rows.

BO rem sts.

Front Neck

Place 15 (16, 17, 18, 19) sts from holder onto needle. With RS facing, join MC.

Row 1 (RS) Knit.

Row 2 Purl.

Dec row BO 2 (3, 3, 3, 3) sts, k to end.

Rep last 2 rows 0 (0, 0, 1, 2) times—13 (13, 14, 12, 10) sts.

Next row Purl.

Dec row BO 2 sts, k to end.

Rep last 2 rows 3 (3, 3, 2, 1) times—5 (5, 6, 6, 6) sts.

Next row Purl.

Dec row K1, ssk, k to end.

Rep last 2 rows 1 (1, 2, 2, 2) times—3 (3, 3, 3, 3) sts.

Work even for 2 (3, 2, 2, 2) rows.

BO rem sts.

RIGHT SLEEVE

Work same as left sleeve, through saddle directions. Divide for neck opening.

Back Neck

Row 1 (WS) P15 (16, 17, 18, 19) and place these sts on holder for back neck; BO 8 CC sts; p to end—15 (16, 17, 18, 19) sts.

Dec row K1, k2tog, k to end.

Rep dec row every other row 2 (2, 2, 3, 3) times more; every 4th row 2 (3, 3, 1, 4) times; then every 6th row 1 (1, 1, 2, 0) times—9 (9, 10, 11, 11) sts. Work even for 3 (1, 1, 1, 1) rows. AT THE SAME TIME, starting with row 21 (23, 23, 23, 23), BO 3 sts at beg of next 2 WS rows.

BO rem sts.

Front Neck

Place 15 (16, 17, 18, 19) sts from holder onto needle. With RS facing, join MC.

Row 1 (RS) Knit.

Dec row BO 2 (3, 3, 3, 3) sts, p to end.

Rep last 2 rows 0 (0, 0, 1, 2) times—13 (13, 14, 12, 10) sts.

Next row Knit.

Dec row BO 2 sts, p to end.

Rep last 2 rows 3 (3, 3, 2, 1) times—5 (5, 6, 6, 6) sts.

Dec row K1, ssk, k to end.

Next row Purl.

Rep last 2 rows 1 (1, 2, 2, 2) times—3 (3, 3, 3, 3) sts.

Work even for 2 (3, 2, 2, 2) rows.

BO rem sts.

FINISHING

Sew sleeves together at back neck and front neck seams.

Pin sleeves to back, matching center point of back with back neck seam. Sew each side of seam, from center back to underarm. Sew front seam as for back. Sew sleeve and side seams.

Neckband

With RS facing, circular needle and MC, starting at center of back neck, PU and k 87 (90, 93, 93, 96) sts evenly around neck opening. Pm and join. Work in p2, k1 rib for 6 rnds. BO in rib.

Weave in ends.

About Joshua I am an artist, designer, and jack-of-all-trades doomed to tinker and dabble in any creative endeavor I can get my hands on. My wife, the mastermind behind KnitWit Yarn Shop in Portland, ME, introduced me to knitting, which first meant I became the willing male mascot and now co-owner of the store. Never satisfied with ready-made patterns, I have a stack of sketches in my studio, next to a bigger stack of swatches. I'm frantically working to keep up with the business and avoid being fired from my post as the yarnshop novelty. Visit us at www.yarnonthebrain.com.

Size

Whiskey: 17" tall

Beer: 16" tall

Materials

Whiskey

A: Lion Brand *Lion Suede* (100% polyester; 85g/122 yd), 1 skein #132 Olive

B: Lion Brand *Wool-Ease* (80% acrylic, 20% wool; 85g/197 yd), 1 skein #138 Cranberry

C: 1 skein #153 Black

D: 1 skein #99 Fisherman

Beer

A: Lion Brand *Lion Suede Prints* (100% polyester; 85g/111 yd), 1 skein #201 Canyon

B: Lion Brand *Wool-Ease* (80% acrylic, 20% wool; 85g/197 yd), 1 skein #102 Ranch Red

C: Lion Brand *Vanna's Choice* (100% acrylic, 100g/170 yd), 1 skein #100 white

D: 1 skein #107 Blue Heather

E: 1 skein #151 Grey Heather

F: 1 skein #111 Navy

US 8 (5mm) straight needles, or size needed to obtain gauge

Sizes H/8 (5mm) and J/10 (6mm) crochet hooks

Poly-fil stuffing

Gauge

17 sts and 19 rows = 4" in St st with A

18 sts and 24 rows = 4" in St st with 2 strands B held tog

MARISA SPASSER

Hangover Helpers

A close friend of mine had recently started working on his Ph.D., and joked that grad school was about learning how to do research and drink heavily. He then asked me if I could knit him a bottle of his favorite whiskey. My mission became to make him the cuddliest bottle of booze I could muster. These pillows, made of thick chenille-like yarn and a wool/acrylic blend, just might be the hair of the dog that a student needs after a night of too much "research," and they're just the right size to be tossed on the couch or the bed. I've included patterns modeled after brands of Irish whiskey and American beer, but feel free to alter the colors for your recipient's drink of choice. They're the ultimate in décor for any frat house.

Chart A

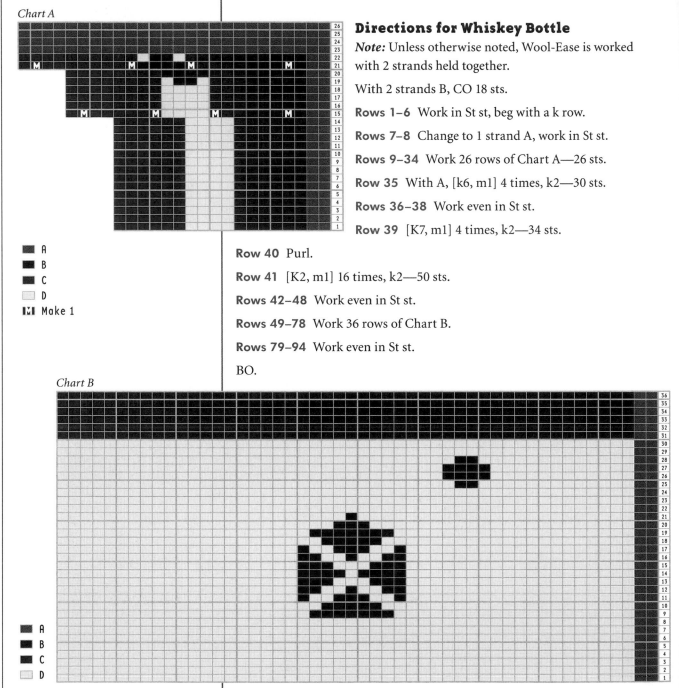

A
B
C
D
Make 1

Directions for Whiskey Bottle

Note: Unless otherwise noted, Wool-Ease is worked with 2 strands held together.

With 2 strands B, CO 18 sts.

Rows 1–6 Work in St st, beg with a k row.

Rows 7–8 Change to 1 strand A, work in St st.

Rows 9–34 Work 26 rows of Chart A—26 sts.

Row 35 With A, [k6, m1] 4 times, k2—30 sts.

Rows 36–38 Work even in St st.

Row 39 [K7, m1] 4 times, k2—34 sts.

Row 40 Purl.

Row 41 [K2, m1] 16 times, k2—50 sts.

Rows 42–48 Work even in St st.

Rows 49–78 Work 36 rows of Chart B.

Rows 79–94 Work even in St st.

BO.

Chart B

A
B
C
D

Cap

With smaller hook and one strand B, ch 2.

Rnd 1 6 sc in 2nd ch from hook, sl st in first sc to join—6 sc.

Rnd 2 Ch 1, 2 sc in each sc around, sl st in turning ch to join—12 sc.

Rnd 3 Ch 1, *2 sc in next sc, 1 sc in next sc; rep from * around, sl st in turning ch to join—18 sts.

Fasten off, leaving a long tail for sewing.

Base

With larger hook and A, ch 2.

Rnds 1–3 Work same as cap.

Rnd 4 Ch 1, *2 sc in next sc, 1 sc in each of next 2 sc; rep from * around, sl st in turning ch to join—24 sts.

Rnd 5 Ch 1, *2 sc in next sc, 1 sc in each of next 3 sc; rep from * around, sl st in turning ch to join—30 sts.

Rnd 6 Ch 1, *2 sc in next sc, 1 sc in each of next 4 sc; rep from * around, sl st in turning ch to join—36 sts.

Rnd 7 Ch 1, *2 sc in next sc, 1 sc in each of next 5 sc; rep from * around, sl st in turning ch to join—42 sts.

Fasten off, leaving a long tail for sewing.

FINISHING

Foll Chart C, embroider text onto label.

With A, sew side seam of bottle. Using ending tail of cap, whip stitch to top of bottle. Stuff bottle with Poly-fil. Using ending tail of base, whip stitch to bottom of bottle.

Chart C

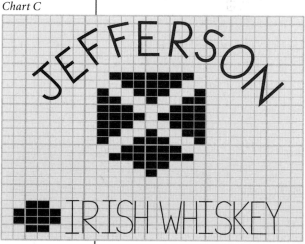

☐ Single strand of C, Backstitch
■ Double strand of C, Backstitch

Chart D

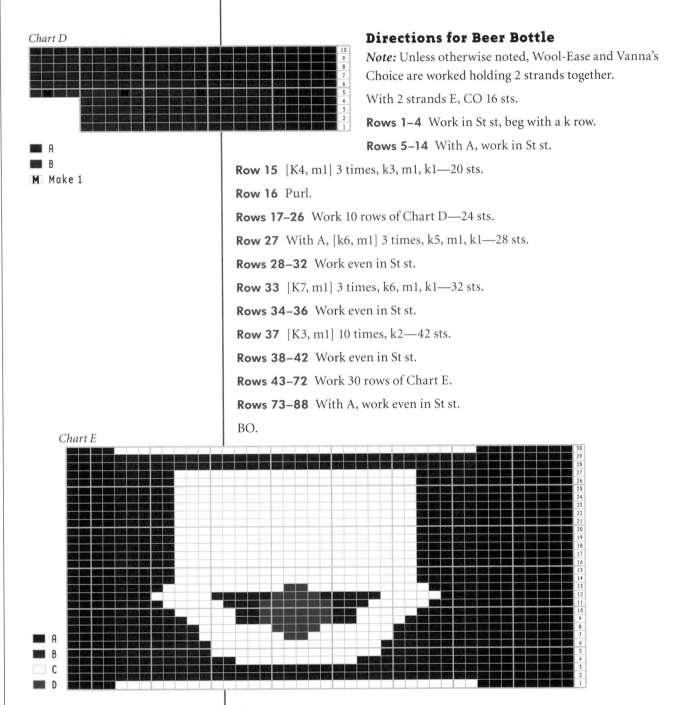

- ■ A
- ■ B
- M Make 1

Directions for Beer Bottle

Note: Unless otherwise noted, Wool-Ease and Vanna's Choice are worked holding 2 strands together.

With 2 strands E, CO 16 sts.

Rows 1–4 Work in St st, beg with a k row.

Rows 5–14 With A, work in St st.

Row 15 [K4, m1] 3 times, k3, m1, k1—20 sts.

Row 16 Purl.

Rows 17–26 Work 10 rows of Chart D—24 sts.

Row 27 With A, [k6, m1] 3 times, k5, m1, k1—28 sts.

Rows 28–32 Work even in St st.

Row 33 [K7, m1] 3 times, k6, m1, k1—32 sts.

Rows 34–36 Work even in St st.

Row 37 [K3, m1] 10 times, k2—42 sts.

Rows 38–42 Work even in St st.

Rows 43–72 Work 30 rows of Chart E.

Rows 73–88 With A, work even in St st.

BO.

Chart E

- ■ A
- ■ B
- □ C
- ■ D

Cap

With smaller hook and one strand E, work same as whiskey cap.

Base

With larger hook and A, work same as whiskey base through Rnd 6—36 sts.

Fasten off, leaving a long tail for sewing.

FINISHING

Foll Charts F and G, embroider text and borders onto labels.

Complete same as whiskey bottle.

Chart F

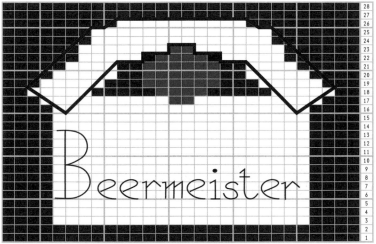

- ▭ Single strand of F, Backstitch
- ▬ Double strand of F, Backstitch
- ⊡ Single strand of F, French knot
- ■ Duplicate stitching with F

Chart G

- ▬ Single strand of C, Backstitch

About Marisa After a friend's mom taught me to knit when I was eight, my knitting knowledge came in dribs and drabs over the years: purling here, casting off there. After a particularly bad holiday season of subjecting friends and family to ridiculous stockinette scarves, I took it upon myself to learn the rest. I plan to move back to my hometown of Chicago some day; in the meantime, I live in a small seaside town in Japan, teaching English and giving impromptu knitting lessons to my students during lunch. I keep track of my various crafting escapades at citruscrafts.blogspot.com.

GARY SKINNER

Look Sharp Socks

I hate making socks. I would rather drive a set of 000 double points into my eyes than make a pair of socks. Yet I loved knitting these, which are constructed using the entrelac method with two wildly contrasting colors of yarn. While they are an interesting project, they do take a bit more time to finish because there are approximately 29,443 stitches to a pair. (Yes, I figured it out.) But I can guarantee you, if you make these socks, people won't just say, "Nice socks!" Instead, they'll go, "Those are the coolest things I've ever seen!" Made with yarn that is a combination of cotton and elastic, they'll stay up like nobody's business, and the care is minimal. Although the yarn manufacturer suggests hand washing, I have a couple of pairs that I routinely throw in the washer and dryer with everything else (except bleach!) and they still are wearing like iron.

Size

Men's medium

Finished circumference: 9"

Materials

Cascade *Fixation* (98.3% cotton, 1.7% elastic; 50g/100 yd)

MC: 1 ball #5806 bright green

CC: 1 ball #8990 black

US 1 (2.25mm) double-pointed needles (set of 5)

Size F/5 (3.75mm) crochet hook for working in ends

Gauge

13 sts and 23 rows = 1½" in entrelac pattern

Directions

CUFF

With MC, CO 52 sts. Divide sts evenly over 4 dpns. Pm and join.

Work in k3, p1 rib for 13 rnds.

Remove marker.

LEG

First Tier of Motifs (Triangles)

Work with MC, starting with Needle 1.

Row 1 (RS) K2, turn.

Row 2 Sl 1, p1, turn.

Row 3 K3, turn.

Row 4 Sl 1, k1, p1, turn.

Row 5 K4, turn.

Row 6 Sl 1, p1, k1, p1, turn.

Row 7 K5, turn.

Row 8 Sl 1, [k1, p1] twice, turn.

Row 9 K6, turn.

Row 10 Sl 1, p1, [k1, p1] twice, turn.

Row 11 K7, turn.

Row 12 Sl 1, [k1, p1] 3 times, turn.

Row 13 K8, turn.

Row 14 Sl 1, p1, [k1, p1] 3 times, turn.

Row 15 K9, turn.

Row 16 Sl 1, [k1, p1] 4 times, turn.

Row 17 K10, turn.

Row 18 Sl 1, p1, [k1, p1] 4 times, turn.

Row 19 K11, turn.

Row 20 Sl 1, [k1, p1] 5 times, turn.

Row 21 K12, turn.

Row 22 Sl 1, p1, [k1, p1] 5 times, turn.

Row 23 K13—one triangle completed.

Rep rows 1–23 on rem 3 needles—4 triangles.

Second Tier of Motifs (Blocks)

This set of blocks will be worked from left to right around circumference of sock (remove marker after cuff).

First Block

Work with CC, starting with triangle on Needle 1.

Row 1 (RS) PU and k13 sts evenly along RH edge of triangle, turn.

Row 2 Sl 1, p1, [k1, p1] 5 times, p2tog (working last st tog with first st on Needle 4), turn.

Row 3 K13, turn.

Rep rows 2 and 3 until all sts on Needle 4 have been worked, ending with a WS row—one CC block on Needle 4, between the last and first triangles. Do not turn after last row.

Second Block

Cont with CC, starting with triangle on Needle 4.

Row 1 (WS) PU and p13 sts evenly along edge of triangle, turn.

Row 2 K13, turn.

Row 3 Sl 1, [k1, p1] 5 times, k1, p2tog (working last st tog with first st on next needle), turn.

Rep rows 2 and 3 until all sts on next needle have been worked, ending with a WS row. Do not turn after last row.

Third and Fourth Blocks

Rep directions for second block on triangles of Needle 3, then Needle 2.

Third Tier of Motifs (Blocks)

This set of blocks is worked from right to left around circumference of sock.

First Block

Work with MC, starting with block on Needle 4.

Row 1 (WS) PU and p13 sts evenly along edge of block, turn.

Row 2 Sl 1, p1, [k1, p1] 5 times, ssk (working last st tog with first st on next needle), turn.

Row 3 P13, turn.

Rep rows 2 and 3 until all sts on next needle have been worked, ending with a RS row—one MC block on Needle 1, between last and first blocks. Do not turn after last row.

Second Block

Row 1 (RS) PU and k13 sts evenly along edge of block, turn.

Row 2 P13, turn.

Row 3 Sl 1, p1, [k1, p1] 5 times, ssk, turn.

Rep rows 2 and 3 until all sts on next needle have been worked. Do not turn after last row.

Third and Fourth Blocks

Rep directions for second block on block of Needle 2, then of Needle 3.

Fourth Tier

Work same as Second tier, picking up sts along sides of blocks instead of triangles.

Fifth and Sixth Tier

Work as est.

Seventh Tier

Work first 2 blocks same as 3rd tier.

HEEL PREP

Instead of 2 complete blocks, make 2 triangles in reverse:

Row 1 (WS) PU and p13 sts evenly along edge of block, turn.

Row 2 Sl 1, p1, [k1, p1] 5 times, ssk (working last st tog with first st on next needle), turn.

Row 3 P12, turn.

Row 4 Sl 1, [k1, p1] 5 times, ssk, turn.

Row 5 P11, turn.

Row 6 Sl 1, p1, [k1, p1] 4 times, ssk, turn.

Row 7 P10, turn.

Row 8 Sl 1, [k1, p1] 4 times, ssk, turn.

Row 9 P9, turn.

Row 10 Sl 1, p1, [k1, p1] 3 times, ssk, turn.

Row 11 P8, turn.

Row 12 Sl 1, [k1, p1] 3 times, ssk, turn.

Row 13 P7, turn.

Row 14 Sl 1, p1, [k1, p1] twice, ssk, turn.

Row 15 P6, turn.

Row 16 Sl 1, [k1, p1] twice, ssk, turn.

Row 17 P5, turn.

Row 18 Sl 1, p1, k1, p1, ssk, turn.

Row 19 P4, turn.

Row 20 Sl 1, k1, p1, ssk, turn.

Row 21 P3, turn.

Row 22 Sl 1, p1, ssk, turn.

Row 23 P2, turn.

Row 24 Sl 1, ssk, turn.

Row 25 P1, turn.

Row 26 Ssk.

One reverse triangle—13 sts.

Rep rows 1–26 in next space to make 2nd reverse triangle.

HEEL

Place 26 sts of the 2 triangles onto one needle. Short-row heel is worked back and forth over these sts.

Row 1 Purl.

Row 2 K24, W&T.

Row 3 P23, W&T.

Row 4 K22, W&T.

Row 5 P21, W&T.

Cont as est, working 1 fewer st before each W&T until there are 12 unwrapped sts.

Next row (RS) K to first wrapped st, PU and k wrap tog with wrapped st, sl 1, turn.

Next row P to next wrapped st, PU and p wrap tog with wrapped st, sl 1, turn.

Next row K to slipped st, PU and k wrap in row below with slipped st, sl 1, turn.

Next row P to slipped st, PU and p wrap in row below with slipped st, sl 1, turn.

Rep last 2 rows until all wraps have been worked.

FOOT PREP

With RS facing and CC, work rows 1–23 of first tier to make 2 triangles on Needles 3 and 4 across 26 heel sts.

FOOT

With MC, work 4th tier. With CC, work 3rd tier. Cont

working tiers in alternating colors until foot meas approx 2½" less than desired finished length to tip of last tier.

With color opposing last tier, work rows 1–26 of heel prep over each needle creating 4 reverse triangles around—52 sts.

TOE

With color opposing triangles, k 13 rnds.

Work toe dec with opposing color from last rnd.

Rnd 1 *K2tog, k22, ssk; rep from * once more.

Rnd 2 Knit.

Rnd 3 *K2tog, k20, ssk; rep from * once more.

Rnd 4 Knit.

Cont as est, working 2 fewer sts between dec every other row until 24 sts rem. Slip first 12 sts onto one needle and last 12 sts onto a 2nd needle.

FINISHING

Graft sts using kitchener st.

Weave in ends.

Make second sock using the opposite color scheme from first sock.

About Gary I was raised in rural New Hampshire, where I attended college and graduated with degrees in mathematics, accounting, and fine arts. I first became interested in knitting at about age twelve; my mom was making me a sweater and I ruined it by carefully pulling it apart so I could understand how yarn could create this fascinating piece of fabric. She taught me how to knit soon after. In my knitting, I never use patterns or instructions. I find it far more exciting to just start something—whatever it may be. In addition to being a knitter, I am an artist living in Seattle who makes money by working in software development, testing, and network engineering.

Size

13"W x 11"H x 5"D after felting

Materials

Knit Picks *Wool of the Andes* (100% wool; 50g/110 yd)

MC: 12 balls #23897 Forest Heather

CC: 2 balls #23432 Cloud

US 13 (9mm) 29" circular needle, or size needed to obtain gauge

Stitch marker

5" by 13" piece of plastic mesh

⅔ yd denim fabric

2 yds of 2" nylon webbing

Two 2" plastic sliders

Gauge

12 sts and 13 rows = 4" in St st with 2 strands held tog (before felting)

STEPHANIE GOURLEY

DJ Bag

There was a time when one could receive no higher compliment from a significant other than a mixtape, a sign of true love indeed. While the mixtape may have been replaced by iPod playlists, the nostalgia of the cassette lives on. Music geeks will love the retro cassette image on the front flap of this bag, then flip upon finding out the bag is sized to hold records! It's perfect for DJs or for anyone who spends too much time at the local music store. It's felted, lined, and has plastic mesh reinforcement to make it able to handle both the weight of vinyl and the punishment of the user. And if your dude's no DJ, just alter the dimensions a bit to fit his laptop or legal files. For lighter duty, the bag can be used without lining or mesh.

Directions

Note: The body of this piece is knit in the round, then the front and sides are bound off and the front flap is knit flat. The bottom piece is knit separately. The entire piece is knit with two strands held together.

BODY

With 2 strands MC held tog, CO 140 sts. K 1 row. Pm and join.

Work even in St st until piece meas 16" from beg. Remove stitch marker.

BO 4 sts.

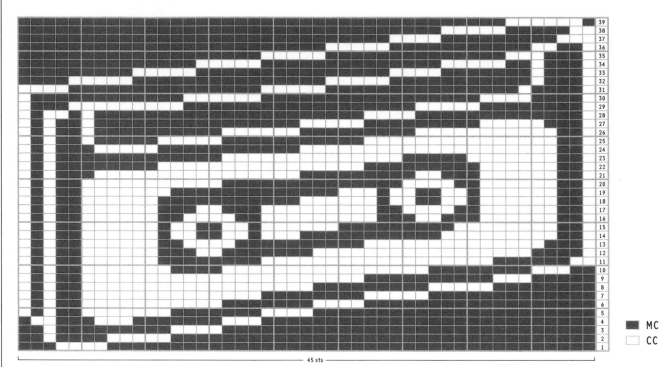

45 sts

■ MC
□ CC

Strap Tab

With 1 st on RH needle, k7—8 sts. Work back and forth in St st on these 8 sts for 10 rows. BO 8 sts and break yarn.

Rejoin yarns to next st on body of bag and BO 62 sts.

Rep from * to *.

Rejoin yarns to next st on body of bag and BO 4 sts—54 sts.

Front Flap

Row 1 Knit.

Row 2 K2, p50, k2.

Rep rows 1 and 2 for 7".

Keeping in patt as est, work 39 rows of chart on center 45 sts.

K 3 rows. BO.

BASE

With 2 strands MC held tog, CO 17 sts. Work even in St st until piece meas 16" from beg. BO.

STRAP PAD

With 2 strands MC held tog, CO 17 sts. Work even in garter st until piece meas 9" from beg. BO.

FINISHING

With RS tog, pin base to bottom opening, taking care to keep front flap centered. Sew base in place. Fold strap pad in half lengthwise and sew seam to form tube. Weave in ends.

To felt, place all pieces in zippered pillowcase and run through hot wash cycle with dish soap and old jeans. Repeat cycle until bag has reached desired size, checking progress every 10 minutes. Wrap in towel and gently

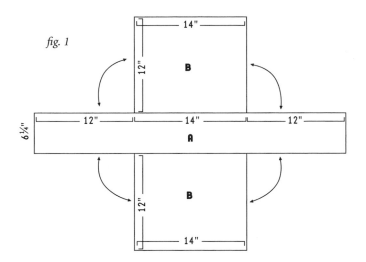

fig. 1

14"

B

12"

12" — 14" — 12"

6¼"

A

12"

B

14"

About Stephanie Since I'm from Arizona, I was not prepared for the cold when I went to college in the Northeast, but my fashion sense told me I desperately needed some legwarmers. My roommate recognized my crafty side and bought me a knitting kit and the obsession began. I now reside in Los Angeles, so my needles tend to churn out more bags than sweaters, but I am always striving to create something unique and usable. I am also a recording engineer, and on really good days, rock stars compliment my knitting.

press out excess water. Place plastic-wrapped records into bag to form to correct size. Air-dry fully in a warm and dry location.

LINING

Cut 4 pieces of fabric as foll:

A 1 pc 6¼" by 38" (sides/base gusset)

B 2 pcs 14" by 12" (front and back)

C 1 pc 15" by 16" (front flap)

Mark centers of long edges on A and B pieces. Pin one B piece to A with RS tog, matching center marks. Sew 3 sides leaving a ½" seam allowance. Repeat with second B piece on opposite side of A (see fig. 1). Stitch the plastic mesh to WS of the base section of A.

Turn under ½" hem on 3 sides of C and sew to inside of front flap.

Place a 5" piece webbing on WS of each strap tab, then slip a 2" plastic slider onto each tab.

Turn under ½" hem on lining and sew in place in bag with WS tog, enclosing end of front flap lining. At sides of opening fold tabs to WS, tuck under lining and sew in place.

Slide strap pad onto 53" length of webbing. Thread each end of webbing through the plastic sliders and sew in place with a 2" overlap.

KIMBERLY FAIRCHILD

Treads

As it stretches out at the calf and tapers to the ankle, the cable and rib patterns on these socks are reminiscent of tire treads—and the wonderfully wooly yarn will keep your guy comfortable wherever he may roam. I designed and knit these socks for my fiancé after we got engaged. The cable is easy to memorize and adds just a small bit of pizzazz. The 100 percent wool yarn is surprisingly soft and warm, and on the small needles it creates a nice dense fabric. These socks are guaranteed to keep your man's feet warm and dry as he treks to work or zooms around town on his motorcycle, and to leave him enough energy to drive you wild when he gets home.

Size

Men's US 11

Foot circumference: 8"

Cuff to heel: 10½"

Foot length: approx 11"

Materials

Dale of Norway *Baby Ull* (100% merino wool; 50g/175m), 4 balls #0083 Charcoal Heather

US 0 (2mm) Two 16" circular needles, or size needed to obtain gauge

5 stitch markers

Cable needle

Gauge

40 sts and 56 rows = 4" in St st

Cable Pattern Chart

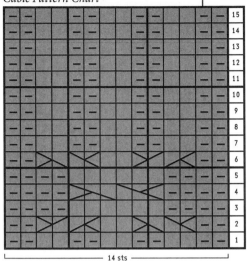

└─── 14 sts ───┘

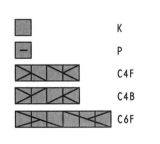

	K
	P
	C4F
	C4B
	C6F

Special abbreviations

W&T (Wrap and turn): On RS, bring yarn between needles to front, sl next st onto RH needle, bring yarn between needles to back, and return sl st to LH needle, turn.

On WS, bring yarn between needles to back, sl next st onto RH needle, bring yarn between needles to front, and return sl st to LH needle, turn.

C4F: Slip 2 sts to cn and hold in front, p2, k2 from cn

C4B: Slip 2 sts to cn and hold in back, k2, p2 from cn

C6F: Slip 3 sts to cn and hold in front, k3, k3 from cn

Directions

Note: These socks are worked over 2 circular needles (see page 65), but feel free to convert the pattern for DPNs.

CUFF

CO 100 sts. Divide evenly over the 2 needles. Pm and join.

Rnds 1–9 *K2, p2; rep from * around.

LEG

Set-up rnd K2, *[p2, k2] 4 times, pm, work 14 sts of cable patt chart, pm, k2, [p2, k2] 8 times, pm, work 14 sts of cable patt chart, pm, [k2, p2] 5 times.

Cont in patt as est until leg meas approx 10" from beg, ending with rnd 3 of patt—8 circles completed. *Note:* One cable will be in the middle of each needle. Ultimately these cables will be on the sides of the leg.

K 10 rnds.

HEEL

Rearrange sts as foll: With Needle 1, k25 (you should be over the center of a cable); with Needle 2, k25 from end of Needle 1 and k23 from Needle 2; then slip last 27 sts of needle 2 onto Needle 1—52 sts on Needle 1 and 48 sts on

Needle 2; center of cables positioned between Needles at sides of sock. Heel is worked on 52 sts of Needle 1.

First Half

Row 1 Working on Needle 1 only, k to last st, W&T.

Row 2 P to last st, W&T.

Row 3 K to 1 st before wrapped st, W&T.

Row 4 P to 1 st before wrapped st, W&T.

Rep rows 3 and 4 until there are 17 wrapped sts on each side of center 18 live sts. The heel should look like a trapezoid.

Second Half

Row 1 K to first wrapped st, PU wrap and k tog with st tbl, W&T (st will have 2 wraps).

Row 2 P to first wrapped st, PU wrap and p tog with st, W&T (st will have 2 wraps).

Rep rows 1 and 2, except PU 2 wraps and working tog with st, until there are 52 live sts again.

FOOT

K even in St st until foot meas 8½" from back of heel or 2½" less than desired finished length.

TOE

Rearrange sts as foll: With Needle 1, k51, sl first and last sts of Needle 1 onto Needle 2—50 sts on each needle. Toe is worked on 50 sts of Needle 2.

Working on Needle 2 only, work same as first half of heel until there are 16 wrapped sts on each side of center 18 live sts; then work as second half of heel until there are 50 live sts again.

FINISHING

Using kitchener st, graft the sts of Needle 1 together with sts of Needle 2. Weave in ends. Block lightly.

About Kimberly In my knitting day-dreams, I'm jetting from gourmet cuisine in New York to dessert and cocktails in Paris, from romantic nights in Venice to days knitting with the finest vicuña wool in Patagonia. In reality, my knitting serves to soothe and relax me during this highly stressful time of writing a dissertation, planning a wedding, working at two universities, and applying for academic jobs. Until my globe-trotting fantasies become reality, I'm satisfied with ordering yarn from exotic locales via the Internet. Keep up with my adventures at drgirlfriend.com.

CLAUDIA LANG

Tubey

If the man in your life is a regular-athletic-sock kinda guy, this is a great pattern for him. While they look like your average, everyday jock socks, they are anything but. Knit in a silky soft hand-dyed merino, they are full of small details that add up to a luxury handmade item for a very special guy. You can knit the stripes in the colors shown here or make them more personal by using the colors of his favorite sports team. They're knit from the cuff down with a traditional heel flap, gussets, and easy toe shaping, which first-time sock knitters will really appreciate. Best of all, they knit up fast—even for big feet, I swear.

Stripe pattern
2 rnds MC, 5 rnds CC1, 3 rnds MC, 10 rnds CC2, 3 rnds MC,
5 rnds CC1, 3 rnds MC.

Directions
Note: The 3-st garter ridge border on the heel is a nice way to end the heel rows and creates an easy edge to later pick up the stitches for the gusset.

CUFF
With MC, CO 72 sts. Divide sts over 3 dpns as foll: 18 (Needle 1), 18 (Needle 2), 36 (Needle 3). Pm and join. Work 31-rnd Stripe patt in k2, p2 rib as foll: K1, *p2, k2; rep from * to last st, k1.

LEG
Work remainder of sock in MC only.

Rnd 1 K1, p2, k30, p2, k2, p2, k30, p2, k1.

Size
Men's US 11

Foot circumference: 9"

Cuff to heel: 7½"

Foot length: approx 10¾"

Materials
Hand Jive *Nature's Palette* (100% merino wool; 50g/185 yd)

MC: 2 skeins #100 Cream

CC1: 1 skein #105 Indian Paintbrush

CC2: 1 skein #108 Acacia

US 0 (2mm) double-pointed needles (set of 4), or size needed to obtain gauge

Gauge
32 sts and 44 rows = 4" in St st

Rep rnd 1 until leg meas 7½" from beg or to desired length, turn.

HEEL

The heel is worked over 36 sts of Needle 3, beginning with a WS row and ending with a RS row.

Flap

Row 1 (WS) K3, p to last 3 sts, k3.

Row 2 K3, *sl 1, k1; rep from * to last 3 sts, k3.

Rep rows 1 and 2 until there are 36 rows in heel flap, ending with a RS row.

Turn Heel

Row 1 (WS) Sl 1, p18, p2tog, p1, turn.

Row 2 Sl 1, k3, ssk, k1, turn.

There will be a small gap between sts of heel turn and unworked sts.

Row 3 Sl 1, p to 1 st before gap, p2tog, p1, turn.

Row 4 Sl 1, k to 1 st before gap, ssk, k1, turn.

Rep rows 3 and 4 until all sts have been worked, ending with a RS row—20 sts.

Heel flap meas approx 2⅜".

Gussets

Renumber needles and rearrange sts as foll: 20 heel sts on Needle 1. With Needle 1 with RS facing, PU and k18 sts along side of heel flap plus 2 sts between heel and instep; Needle 2, k36 across instep; Needle 3, PU and k 2 sts between instep and heel plus 18 along side of heel flap and k10 from Needle 1—96 sts. Pm for new beg of rnd. K 1 rnd.

Shape Gussets

Rnd 1 Needle 1, k to last 2 sts, ssk; Needle 2, knit; Needle 3, k2tog, k to end.

Rnd 2 Needle 1, k to last 3 sts, ssk, k1; Needle 2, knit; Needle 3, k1, k2tog, k to end.

Rnd 3 Knit.

Rep rnds 2 and 3 until there are 72 sts.

FOOT

Work even in St st until foot meas 8¾" from back of heel or 2" less than desired finished length.

TOE

Rnd 1 Needle 1, k to last 3 sts, k2tog, k1; Needle 2, k1, ssk, k to last 3 sts, k2tog, k1; Needle 3, k1, ssk, k to end.

Rnd 2 Knit.

Rep rnds 1 and 2 until there are 36 sts.

Rep rnd 1 until there are 20 sts.

Cont with Needle 3, k5 from Needle 1.

Graft toe sts using kitchener st.

FINISHING

Weave in ends, and block to shape.

About Claudia I was born and raised in Bavaria, Germany, and moved to the United States in 2000 to join my boyfriend—now my husband—in the suburbs of Atlanta, GA. My mom taught me how to knit when I was ten years old, and knitting has been a part of my life ever since. Here in the U.S., my knitting has taken on new dimensions. Techniques such as felting and lace-making have joined my old favorites, and recently I added spinning to my repertoire. I am a member of the Atlanta Knitting Guild and the Peachtree Handspinners Guild, as well as the SnB Group in Atlanta, and as time permits, I teach knitting classes. Besides all this, I have a full-time job. You can read about my fiber adventures on my blog, "Knitting Without Doghair Is Not an Option," at www.bavgirl.com.

Size

Approx 38–46", customizable to the vehicle. The circumference of the steering wheel will be equal to the stretched length of your knitting.

Materials

Berroco Suede (100% nylon; 50g/120 yd)

MC: 2 balls #3729 Zorro

CC: 1 ball #3751 Miss Kitty

US 6 (4mm) straight needles

Cable needle

Stitch markers

WENDY RAVINSKI

Wheel on Fire

This steering wheel cover is made using an intarsia and cable pattern, producing a red flame effect against the black background. The suede yarn is soft luxury for the fingers. It grips nicely against the wheel, and the cable adds the perfect texture for gripping as you drive. On a sizzling summer day, your Wheel on Fire will be hot in looks but not in touch. The cover could also be made in a single color with a cable down the center that conforms to the driver's fingers, or you could customize the color of the suede for his vehicle.

Special abbreviation

C8F: Sl 4 st to cn and hold in front, k4, k4 from ch.

Directions

Note: The steering wheel cover is knit in intarsia in one long stretch like a scarf, with the cable being the contrast color. I stretch it while measuring, as I want the cover to be as tight as possible to prevent slipping. Twist yarns on WS when changing colors to prevent holes.

CO 8 sts MC, 8 sts CC, 8 sts with 2nd ball MC—24 sts.

Row 1 (WS) With MC, k2, p4, k2; with CC, p8; with MC, k2, p4, k2.

Row 2 With MC, k6, p2; with CC, k8; with MC, p2, k6.

Rows 3, 5 and 7 Rep row 1.

Row 4 With MC, k6, p2; with CC, C8F; with MC, p2, k6.

Rows 6 and 8 Rep row 2.

Rep rows 1–8 to desired stretched length, approx 38", leaving sts on needle.

FINISHING

Break off yarn, leaving a long tail. Sew or graft sts to CO edge. Weave in ends. Fold garter st borders to WS, stretch cover around steering wheel and whipstitch sides together, around wheel, taking care to make stitches between braces of wheel to prevent slippage while driving.

About Wendy I'm the mother of two beautiful girls and the wife of a husband who encourages and supports my passion for the fiber arts. I learned to knit as a child, but quickly forgot it. Then a few years ago, inspired by a baby blanket a friend made for one of my daughters, I decided to reteach myself with the help of the Internet. Now I teach others to crochet and knit. I also spin fiber and dabble in knit and crochet pattern design. My other hobbies include photography, quilting, scrapbooking, gardening, and keeping a blog at earthwhisperfiberarts.com.

Size

Men's medium

Finished circumference: 8"

Cuff to heel: 7½"

Foot length: Adjustable

Materials

Brown Sheep *Wildfoote* Luxury Sock Yarn
(75% wool, 25% nylon; 50g/215 yd)

MC: 2 skeins #SY26 Blue Blood Red

CC1: 1 skein #SY05 Black Orchid

CC2: 1 skein #SY10 Vanilla

US 1 (2.25mm) straight needles and double-
pointed needles (set of 4)

Gauge

32 sts and 40 rows = 4" in St st

DEBBIE STOLLER

Lucky Socks

When a man's facing a dicey situation, he's got to feel his best from his head down to his toes, and these socks will take care of that last part. Knit in a washable wool-and-nylon blend, they're just the thing for a day at the races, an important meeting with the boss, or a night out on the town. The dice show lucky number 7 in every direction, and they're slyly knit into the leg using the intarsia and Fair Isle methods together, working back and forth on straight needles. After that, you go on in the round, seaming up the leg at the end. The "afterthought" heel is added on at the end, too, which means you can easily replace it if it ever wears out. They're fun to knit, hard-wearing, and practically guarantee the wearer all kinds of Vegas-style luck. It's a win-win situation.

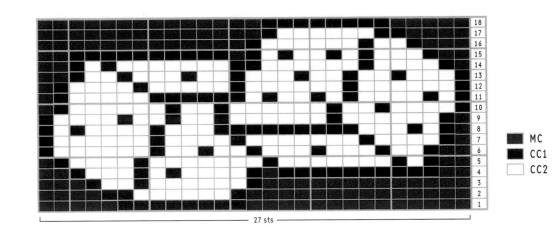

18
17
16
15
14
13
12
11
10
9
8
7
6
5
4
3
2
1

■ MC
■ CC1
□ CC2

—— 27 sts ——

Directions

Note: When working the Dice Chart, both the intarsia and Fair Isle (stranded) methods are used. Cut 18" strands of yarn for the various color portions and twist the MC and CC1 strands around each other at the edges of each motif. Then knit the centers carrying all but the MC strands across each row and catching the unused color every 3 or 4 stitches.

LEG

Using CC1 and straight needles, CO 66 sts *loosely*.

Work back and forth in k1, p1 rib for 20 rows.

Row 1 With MC, knit.

Row 2 With CC2, purl.

Row 3 With CC1, knit.

Rows 4–6 With MC, work in St st.

Right sock only:

Row 7 K3, pm, work chart over next 27 sts, pm, k to end.

Left sock only:

Row 7 K36, pm, work chart over next 27 sts, pm, k to end.

Both socks:

Rows 8–25 Cont in St st, working chart between markers.

Row 26 (WS) With MC, purl.

Row 27 K2tog, k to last 2 sts, k2tog—64 sts.

Distribute sts over 3 dpns as foll: First 16 sts on Needle 1, center 32 sts on Needle 2, last 16 sts on Needle 3.

Pm and join. With MC, work even in St st until leg meas 8" from CO edge.

Preparation row for afterthought heel With MC, k across Needle 1; with wy, k across Needle 2; with MC, k across Needle 2 again; with MC, k across Needle 3— 64 sts.

FOOT

Cont in St st until foot (from wy to needles) meas 4" less than desired length.

TOE

With CC1, k 1 rnd; with CC2, k 1 rnd; with MC, k 1 rnd.

Work remainder of toe with CC1 only.

Rnd 1 Needle 1, k to last 3 sts, k2tog, k1; Needle 2, k1, ssk, k to last 3 sts, k2tog, k1; Needle 3, k1, ssk, k to end.

Rnd 2 Knit.

Rep rnds 1 and 2 until 40 sts rem.

Rep rnd 1 only until 16 sts rem.

With Needle 3, k sts on Needle 1—8 sts on each of 2 needles.

Graft toe sts tog using kitchener st.

AFTERTHOUGHT HEEL

Gently pull wy from sts, leaving a total of 63 live sts. Starting at RH edge of opening, on the side closest to the leg, sl first 16 sts onto Needle 1, next 16 sts onto Needle 2, rem 31 sts onto Needle 3.

With CC1, k across sts on Needles 1 and 2; m1 between Needles 2 and 3, then k across sts on Needle 3—64 sts.

With CC2, k 1 rnd; with MC, k 1 rnd.

Work rem of heel with CC1 only.

Rnd 1 Needle 1, k1, ssk, k to end; Needle 2, k to last 3 sts, k2tog, k1; Needle 3, k1, ssk, k to last 3 sts, k2tog, k1.

Rnd 2 Knit.

Rep rnds 1 and 2 until 32 sts rem.

Rep rnd 1 only until 16 sts rem.

Slip sts from Needle 2 onto Needle 1—8 sts on each of 2 needles.

Graft heel sts together using kitchener st.

FINISHING

Sew back of leg seam, taking care to match stripes.

Weave in ends.

Block.

CATHERINE SERBOUSEK

Tie Me Up, Tie Me Down

I hate my office job. I hate your office job. That feeling of being confined by the yoke of corporate culture never lets up. I thumb my nose at the grindstone and I say why not knit a subversive tie for your boyfriend, thereby sidestepping the curse-of-the-boyfriend altogether! Neckties are one way men can express themselves in silly, obscure, and sometimes even lewd ways. Made in unbusinesslike hemp, these hand-knit ties feature skull and robot motifs. You might even want to knit one at work under your desk; I did. (The trick is to have some paperwork open in front of you and a stool about knee high to place your yarn on!)

Directions

Note: This tie is knit from the bottom (wide end) up. Slip the first stitch of every row and purl the last stitch of every row to minimize curling.

With MC (A), CO 3 sts.

Row 1 Knit.

Row 2 P1, m1, p to last st, m1, p1.

Row 3 K1, m1, k to last st, m1, k1.

Row 4 Purl.

Row 5 K1, m1, k to last st, m1, k1.

Row 6 P1, m1, p to last st, m1, p1—11 sts.

Row 7 Knit.

Size

Finished width: 3½" at its widest point and 1½" at its narrowest

Finished length: 58½" from tip to tip

Materials

Lanaknits *allhemp6* (100% hemp; 100g/165 yd)

Skull

MC: 2 skeins Sprout

CC: 1 skein Pearl

Robot

A: 2 skeins Deep Sea

B: 1 skein Brick

C: 1 skein Pumpkin

D: 1 skein Dijon

E: 1 skein Charcoal

F: 1 skein Foggy

G: 1 skein Sprout

US 3 (3.25mm) straight needles

Retro fabric for backing

Sewing needle and matching thread

Gauge

22 sts and 28 rows = 4" in St st

Rows 8–13 Rep rows 2–7—19 sts.

Row 14 P1, m1, p17, m1, p1—21 sts.

Row 15 Knit.

Row 16 CO 10 sts, p to end (left flap).

Row 17 CO 10 sts, k to end (right flap)—41 sts.

Row 18 Purl.

Work 18 (29) rows of Skull (Robot) Chart over center 19 (19) sts, AT THE SAME TIME shaping tie as foll:

Rows 19–37 Work in St st.

Row 38 P10, p2tog, p17, p2tog, p10—39 sts.

Rows 39–62 Work in St st.

Row 63 K9, k2tog, k17, k2tog, k9—37 sts.

Rows 64–84 Work in St st.

Row 85 K8, k2tog, k17, k2tog, k8—35 sts.

Rows 86–102 Work in St st.

Row 103 K7, k2tog, k17, k2tog, k7—33 sts.

Rows 104–124 Work in St st.

Row 125 K6, k2tog, k17, k2tog, k6—31 sts.

Rows 126–139 Work in St st.

Row 140 P5, p2tog, p17, p2tog, p5—29 sts.

Row 141–164 Work in St st.

Row 165 K4, k2tog, k17, k2tog, k4—27 sts.

Rows 166–174 Work in St st.

Row 175 K3, k2tog, k17, k2tog, k3—25 sts.

Rows 176–179 Work in St st.

Row 180 P2, p2tog, p17, p2tog, p2—23 sts.

Row 181 K1, k2tog, k17, k2tog, k1—21 sts.

Skull Chart

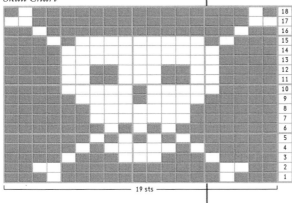

19 sts

■ MC
□ CC

Rows 182–184 Work in St st.

Row 185 K2tog, k17, k2tog—19 sts.

Rows 186–400 Work in St st.

Row 401 BO 4 sts, k to end—15 sts.

Row 402 BO 4 sts, p to end—11 sts.

Row 403 K2tog, k7, k2tog—9 sts.

Row 404 Purl.

Row 405 K2tog, k5, k2tog—7 sts.

Row 406 Purl.

Row 407 K2tog, k3, k2tog—5 sts.

Row 408 Purl.

Row 409 K2tog, k1, k2tog—3 sts.

Break yarn. Thread through rem sts and fasten securely.

FINISHING

For robot, add duplicate stitching detail according to chart.

Block tie with right and left flaps folded under. Cut fabric for lining to cover 14" at wide end and 3" at narrow end of tie, adding a ¼" seam allowance and leaving edge sts exposed for seam. With sewing needle and thread, sew lining in place using a small running st, making sure sts don't show on RS. Sew seam along entire length. Starch and iron.

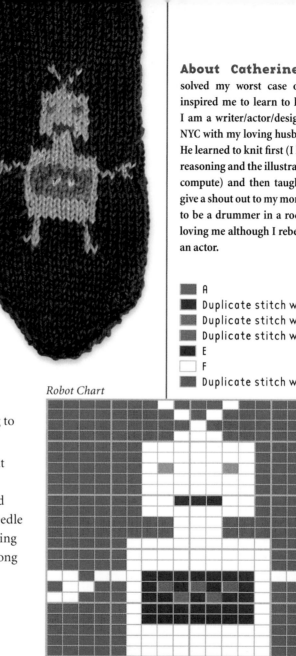

About Catherine A dream that solved my worst case of writer's block inspired me to learn to knit and crochet. I am a writer/actor/designer who lives in NYC with my loving husband who's a chef. He learned to knit first (I have poor spatial reasoning and the illustrations just did not compute) and then taught me. I'd like to give a shout out to my mom for wanting me to be a drummer in a rock band and still loving me although I rebelled and became an actor.

▨ A
▨ Duplicate stitch with B
▨ Duplicate stitch with C
▨ Duplicate stitch with D
▨ E
☐ F
▨ Duplicate stitch with G

Robot Chart

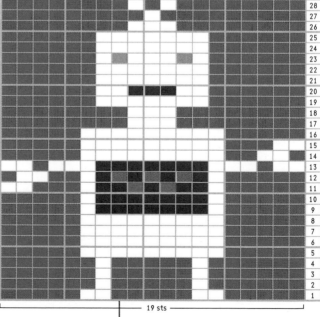

← 19 sts →

ARWYN YARWOOD-HOEPPNER
Deady Bear

This stuffed bear really is stuffed—as in taxidermy. His "X" eyes make it clear that the bee that stung him (and remains stuck in his body, leaving a pool of blood) did him in. But no matter. Even in death, he's still super-cuddly and ready to shock friends and family whether he's perched on a pillow or displayed on a shelf. Perfect for the urban toy collector in your life, he's a pretty quick knit, and the parts aren't terribly difficult to seam up. If you have the appropriate colors on hand, he's also an excellent stash-busting exercise.

Special abbreviations

SSP: Slip two stitches knitwise onto right needle, insert left needle into front loops, purl through back loops

WW: Work wrap together with wrapped stitch

Directions for Bee
BODY AND HEAD

With C, CO 16 sts. Divide sts evenly over 4 dpns, pm and join.

Rnds 1–3 With C, knit.

Rnd 4 With F, *k4, m1; rep from * 3 times more—20 sts.

Rnds 5–6 With F, knit.

Rnd 7 With C, *k5, m1; rep from * 3 times more—24 sts.

Rnds 8–9 With C, knit.

Rnd 10 With F, *k6, m1; rep from * 3 times more—28 sts.

Rnds 11–12 With F, knit.

Size

Approx 13"W x 17"L x 10"H

Materials

Brown Sheep *Nature Spun* (100% wool; 100g/245 yd)

A: 1 skein #N89 Roasted Coffee (divide into two balls)

B: 1 skein #N93 Latte

C: 1 skein #601 Pepper

D: 1 skein #115 Bit of Blue

E: 1 skein #N44 Husker Red

F: 1 skein #305 Impasse Yellow

US 7 (4.5mm) straight and double-pointed needles (set of 5)

US 13 (9mm) straight needles

Stitch holder or waste yarn

Polyester fiberfill

Gauge

18 sts and 24 rows = 4" in St st

Rnds 13–14 With C, knit.

Rnd 15 With C, *k5, k2tog; rep from * 3 times more—24 sts.

Rnds 16–17 With F, knit.

Rnd 18 With F, *k4, k2tog; rep from * 3 times more—20 sts.

Break off F, cont with C only.

Rnds 19–20 Knit.

Rnd 21 *K3, k2tog; rep from * 3 times more—16 sts.

Rnds 22, 24 and 26 Knit.

Rnd 23 *K2, k2tog; rep from * 3 times more—12 sts.

Rnd 25 *K2, m1; rep from * 5 times more—18 sts.

Rnd 27 *K3, m1; rep from * 5 times more—24 sts.

Rnds 28–30 Knit.

Rnd 31 *K2, k2tog; rep from * 5 times more—18 sts.

Rnd 32 *K1, k2tog; rep from * 5 times more—12 sts.

Rnd 33 Knit.

Rnd 34 *K2tog; rep from * around—6 sts.

Break yarn and thread tail through rem sts. Pull tightly to close opening and sew to secure.

LEGS (MAKE 6)

With C and dpns, CO 3 sts. Work in I-cord for 12 rnds. Break yarn and thread tail through sts to finish. Attach to C stripes of body, starting at rnds 1–3.

WINGS (MAKE 2)

Wings are worked on size 13 needles to give a more veined and lacy appearance.

With D and larger needles, CO 4 sts.

Rows 1 and 2 Knit.

Row 3 K1, m1, k2, m1, k1—6 sts.

Rows 4–10 Knit.

Row 11 Ssk, k2, k2tog—4 sts.

Rows 12–14 Knit.

Row 15 Ssk, k2tog—2 sts.

Row 16 Knit.

BO.

Using whipstitch, attach a wing to each side of body above first set of legs.

Directions for Bear

FEET (MAKE 2)

With B, CO 6 sts.

Row 1 Knit.

Row 2 P1, m1, p4, m1, p1—8 sts.

Rows 3, 5 and 7 Knit.

Row 4 P1, m1, p6, m1, p1—10 sts.

Rows 6, 8 and 10 Purl.

Row 9 Ssk, k6, k2tog—8 sts.

Row 11 Ssk, k4, k2tog—6 sts.

BO.

LEGS (MAKE 2)

With RS facing and A, PU and k23 sts around edge of foot. Do not join.

Rows 1, 3 and 5 (WS) Purl.

Rows 2 and 4 Knit.

Row 6 K5, m1, k5, m1, k3, m1, k5, m1, k5—27 sts.

Row 7 and all WS rows Purl.

Rows 8 and 10 Knit.

Row 12 K6, m1, k6, m1, k3, m1, k6, m1, k6—31 sts.

Rows 14 and 16 Knit.

Row 18 K7, m1, k7, m1, k3, m1, k7, m1, k7—35 sts.

Row 20 Knit.

Row 21 Purl.

Break yarn leaving a 6" tail. Place sts on holder. Make 2nd leg; do not break yarn.

BODY

Row 1 Knit across sts of 2nd leg, then cont across sts of first leg—70 sts.

Rows 2 and 4 Purl.

Row 3 Knit.

Row 5 K32 A, k6 B, join 2nd ball of A and k32 A.

Row 6 P32 A, p6 B, p32 A.

Rows 7, 9, 11 and 13 With A, k31, m1; with B, k to last 31 sts; with A, m1, k31.

Rows 8, 10, 12 and 14 With A, p31, m1; with B, p to last 31 sts; with A, m1, p31—86 sts after row 14.

Row 15 With A, k31, m1; k24 B; with A, m1, k31—88 sts.

Row 16 With A, p32, m1; p24 B; with A, m1, p32—90 sts.

Row 17 With A, k33, m1; k24 B; with A, m1, k33—92 sts.

Row 18 P34 A, p24 B, p34 A.

Row 19 With A, k32, ssk; k24 B; with A, k2tog, k32—90 sts.

Row 20 With A, p31, ssp; p24 B; with A, p2tog, p31—88 sts.

Row 21 With A, k31, ssk; k22 B; with A, k1, k2tog, k30—86 sts.

Row 22 With A, p30, ssp, p1; p20 B; with A, p2tog, p31—84 sts.

Row 23 With A, k31, ssk; k18 B; with A, k1, k2tog, k30—82 sts.

Row 24 With A, p30, ssp, p1; p16 B; with A, p2tog, p31—80 sts.

Row 25 With A, k31, ssk; k14 B; with A, k1, k2tog, k30—78 sts.

Row 26 With A, p30, ssp, p1; p12 B; with A, p2tog, p31—76 sts.

Row 27 With A, k31, ssk; k10 B; with A, k1, k2tog, k30—74 sts.

Row 28 With A, p30, ssp, p1; p8 B; with A, p2tog, p31—72 sts.

Row 29 With A, k31, ssk; k6 B; with A, k1, k2tog, k30—70 sts.

Row 30 P32 A; p6 B; p32 A.

Row 31 Cont with A only, knit.

Row 32 and all WS rows Purl.

Row 33 K4, ssk, [k8, ssk] 3 times, [k8, k2tog] 3 times, k4—63 sts.

Row 35 K4, ssk, [k7, ssk] 3 times, [k7, k2tog] 3 times, k3—56 sts.

Row 37 K3, ssk, [k6, ssk] 3 times, [k6, k2tog] 3 times, k3—49 sts.

Row 39 K3, ssk, [k5, ssk] 3 times, [k5, k2tog] 3 times, k2—42 sts.

Begin Head

Row 41 Knit.

Row 43 K7, m1, k14, m1, k14, m1, k7—45 sts.

Row 45 K7, m1, k15, m1, k15, m1, k7—48 sts.

Row 47 K8, m1, k16, m1, k16, m1, k8—51 sts.

Row 49 K8, m1, k17, m1, k17, m1, k8—54 sts.

Row 51 K9, m1, k18, m1, k18, m1, k9—57 sts.

Row 53 K9, m1, k19, m1, k19, m1, k10—60 sts.

Row 55 Knit.

Row 57 K9, ssk, k18, ssk, k18, k2tog, k9—57 sts.

Row 59 K9, ssk, k17, ssk, k17, k2tog, k8—54 sts.

Row 61 K8, ssk, k16, ssk, k16, k2tog, k8—51 sts.

Row 63 K8, ssk, k15, ssk, k15, k2tog, k7—48 sts.

Row 65 K7, ssk, k14, ssk, k14, k2tog, k7—45 sts.

Row 67 K7, ssk, k13, ssk, k13, k2tog, k6—42 sts.

Row 69 K2, ssk, [k4, ssk] 3 times, [k4, k2tog] 3 times, k2—35 sts.

Row 71 K2, ssk, [k3, ssk] 3 times, [k3, k2tog] 3 times, k1—28 sts.

Row 73 K1, ssk, [k2, ssk] 3 times, [k2, k2tog] 3 times, k1—21 sts.

Row 75 K1, ssk, [k1, ssk] 3 times, [k1, k2tog] 3 times—14 sts.

Row 77 [K2tog] 7 times—7 sts.

Break yarn, leaving a long tail for sewing. Thread tail through rem sts. Pull tightly to close opening and sew head seam. Stuff head and body, sewing seam as you stuff. Stuff legs and sew leg seams.

HANDS (MAKE 2)

With B, CO 4 sts.

Row 1 Knit.

Row 2 P1, m1, p2, m1, p1—6 sts.

Rows 3, 5 and 7 Knit.

Row 4 P1, m1, p4, m1, p1—8 sts.

Rows 6, 8 and 10 Purl.

Row 9 Ssk, k4, k2tog—6 sts.

Row 11 Ssk, k2, k2tog—4 sts.

BO purlwise.

ARMS (MAKE 2)

With RS facing and A, leaving a long tail for sewing, PU and k19 sts around edge of hand. Do not join.

Rows 1–13 Work in St st.

Row 14 (RS) Ssk, ssk, k11, k2tog, k2tog—15 sts.

Rows 15, 17, 19 and 21 Purl.

Row 16 Ssk, ssk, k7, k2tog, k2tog—11 sts.

Row 18 Ssk, ssk, k3, k2tog, k2tog—7 sts.

Row 20 Ssk, k3, k2tog—5 sts.

BO.

With beg tail, sew arm seams to row 14. Stuff and sew to side of body, just below head.

MUZZLE

With B, CO 10 sts.

Row 1 Knit.

Row 2 and all WS rows Purl.

Rows 3, 5 and 7 K2, m1, k5, m1, k3—12 sts.

Row 5 K3, m1, k6, m1, k3—14 sts.

Row 7 K3, m1, k7, m1, k4—16 sts.

Row 9 K3, ssk, k6, k2tog, k3—14 sts.

Row 11 K2, ssk, k5, k2tog, k3—12 sts.

Row 13 K2, ssk, k4, k2tog, k2—10 sts.

Row 17 K2, ssk, k3, k2tog, k1—8 sts.

Row 19 K1, ssk k2, k2tog, k1—6 sts.

BO.

Center muzzle over increase line at front of head with CO edge at bottom. Sew in place, stuffing as you go.

TAIL

With B, CO 12 sts.

Row 1 Knit.

Row 2 Purl.

Row 3 K6, W&T, p1, W&T, k2 WW, W&T, p3 WW, W&T, k4 WW, W&T, p5 WW, W&T, k6 WW, W&T, p7 WW, W&T, k8 WW, W&T, p9 WW, W&T, k10 WW, W&T, p11 WW.

Row 4 K1, ssk, k1, ssk, k2tog, k1, k2tog, k1 WW—8 sts.

Row 5 P2tog, p2tog, ssp, ssp—4 sts.

BO.

Center tail over back seam above legs with CO edge on top. Sew in place, stuffing as you go.

EARS (MAKE 4)

With B, CO 10 sts.

Rows 1 and 3 Knit.

Rows 2, 4 and 6 Purl.

Row 5 Ssk, k6, k2tog—8 sts.

Row 7 Ssk, k4, k2tog—6 sts.

BO purlwise.

Place 2 pieces with WS together. Sew around edges to make one ear. Rep with rem 2 pieces. Sew ears to top of head.

BLOOD
Short Stream
With E, CO 4 sts.

Row 1 Knit.

Rows 2, 4 and 6 Purl.

Rows 3, 5 and 7 K1, m1, k to last st, m1, k1—10 sts after row 7.

Row 8 Knit.

Place sts on holder.

Long Stream
With E, CO 3 sts.

Row 1 Knit.

Row 2 and all WS rows Purl.

Row 3 K1, m1, k1, m1, k1—5 sts.

Row 5 K1, m1, k3, m1, k1—7 sts.

Row 7 Ssk, k3, k2tog—5 sts.

Row 9 Knit.

Row 11 Ssk, k1, k2tog—3 sts.

Rows 13, 15, 17, 19 and 21 Knit.

Rows 23, 25, 27 and 29 K1, m1, k to end—7 sts after row 29.

Main Pool
Row 1 With 7 sts of long stream on needle, cont to k10 sts of short stream—17 sts.

Row 2 and all WS rows Purl.

Rows 3 and 5 Knit.

Rows 7 and 9 Ssk, k to last 2 sts, [m1, k1] twice—19 sts after row 9.

Rows 11 and 13 Ssk, k to last 2 sts, k2tog—15 sts after row 13.

Rows 15 and 17 K to last 2 sts, k2tog—13 sts after row 17.

Row 19 Ssk, k9, k2tog—11 sts.

Row 21 Ssk, k5, k2tog, k2tog—8 sts.

Row 23 Ssk, k2, k2tog, k2tog—5 sts.

BO purlwise.

FINISHING
Sew blood to front of body, with main pool over the tummy and long stream down one leg.

With C, embroider nose and mouth on bear's muzzle, sew "X"s for eyes. Stuff bee and sew seam. Sew stinger end of bee to center of blood pool.

About Arwyn Despite the morbid nature of this toy, I love animals of all kinds, and have owned everything from a horse to anole lizards and frogs. My family, which is into various forms of crafting, started me off young with embroidery. From there I branched into many other crafts, but knitting is relatively new to me—I just started that a few years ago. I'm an art school dropout turned stay-at-home-mom of two daughters, but I plan to start working soon as a medical transcriptionist. To read more about my crafting, as well as about my (and my husband's) adventures in parenting and in nerddom, you can find me at angelus49.livejournal.com.

KELLY LADWIG

Lucha Libre

This mask was designed for my son, who brought home a packing list for a winter campout that included a wool balaclava. The only one we had was old, acrylic, and unraveling. Using the old one as a model, I attempted to design a new one with my son's input so it would meet three criteria: It could not be too uncool to pack, unpack, or wear; it had to be comfortable; and it had to be warm, too. I made a number of attempts, and this masquadore mask is the final version of our design. Not only does my son love it, but it's been a hit with every male who's seen it, from the guy at the UPS counter to the four-year-old boys in the class I teach. It's made in face-friendly super-soft merino wool, great colors, and is a fun, quick knit. You'll have lots of inquiries about what you are making with this project.

Directions

Using smaller needles and MC, CO 82 sts.

Row 1 *K2, p2; rep from * to last 2 sts, k2.

Row 2 *P2, k2; rep from * to last 2 sts, p2.

Work in k2, p2 rib for 3", ending with a WS row.

Next row *K2, p2, k1, kfb, [p2, k2] twice, p2, k1, kfb, p2; rep from * 3 times more, k2—90 sts.

Size

One size fits all

Finished circumference: 19½"

Finished length: 14"

Materials

Karabella *Aurora 8* (100% extrafine merino wool; 50g/98 yd)

MC: 2 balls #15 royal blue or #12 green

CC: 1 ball #1250 white or #36 yellow

US 7 (4.5mm) straight needles, or size needed to obtain gauge

US 5 (3.75mm) straight needles

Size F/5 (3.75mm) crochet hook

Ten stitch markers

Gauge

18 sts and 26 rows in St st = 4"

Change to larger needles, work 14 rows in St st.

Work 35 rows of chart over center 34 sts as foll:

Row 1 (RS) K28 MC, pm, k34 sts of chart, pm, k28 MC.

Row 2 Cont in chart patt, purl.

Row 3 K37, join 2nd ball of CC and BO 16 sts, k to end.

Row 4 Working both sides at the same time, purl.

Row 5 K37, cable CO 16 sts, k37.

Rows 6–17 Cont in St st.

Row 18 P32, BO 26 sts, p to end.

Rows 19–23 Working both sides at the same time, work in St st.

Row 24 P32, cable CO 26 sts, p32.

Rows 25–35 Cont in St st.

Cont even with MC in St st until piece meas 12" from beg, ending with a WS row.

SHAPE CROWN

Row 1 *K6, k2tog, pm, k1; rep from * 9 times more—80 sts.

Row 2 Purl.

Row 3 *K to 2 sts before marker, k2tog; rep from * 9 times more—70 sts.

Row 4 Purl.

Rep rows 3 and 4 three times more—40 sts, then rep row 3 once—30 sts.

Next row *P2tog; rep from * to end—15 sts.

Next row *K2tog; rep from * to last st, k1—8 sts.

Break yarn, leaving a long tail.

FINISHING

Using crochet hook and CC, single crochet evenly around mouth opening, making 1 single crochet into each side of mouth. Mark center top and bottom of eye opening. Starting at top marker, single crochet around opening, making 5 single crochets into each side, then slip st into single crochet at lower marker to complete. Fasten off.

Thread tail at crown through rem sts twice and sew back seam.

Weave in ends.

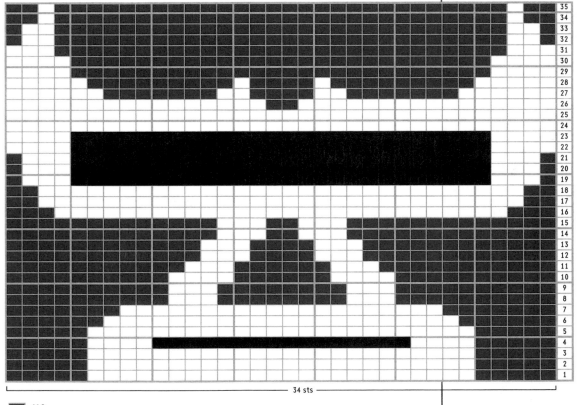

34 sts

- ■ MC
- □ CC
- ▬ mouth and eye opening

Resource Guide

Alchemy Yarns of Transformation
P.O. Box 1080
Sebastopol, CA 95473
www.alchemyyarns.com
707-823-3276

Berroco
P.O. Box 367
14 Elmdale Rd.
Uxbridge, MA 01569
www.berroco.com
508-278-2527

Blue Sky Alpacas
P.O. Box 88
Cedar, MN 55011
www.blueskyalpacas.com
888-460-8862

Brown Sheep Company, Inc.
100662 County Rd. 16
Mitchell, NE 69357
www.brownsheep.com
800-826-9136

Cascade Yarns
1224 Andover Park East
Tukwila, WA 98188
www.cascadeyarns.com
206-574-0440

Classic Elite Yarns, Inc.
122 Western Ave.

Lowell, MA 01851
www.classiceliteyarns.com
978-453-2837

Cleckheaton
Distributed by Plymouth Yarn Co., Inc.
www.cleckheaton.biz

Dale of Norway, Inc.
4570 Shelburne Rd., Ste. 20
Shelburne, VT 05482
www.daleofnorway.com
802-383-0132

Fable Handknit
5143 Tomken Rd.
Mississauga, ON L4W 1P1
Canada
www.fablehandknit.com
905-238-0388

Hemp for Knitting
320 Vernon St., Ste. 3B
Nelson, BC 41L 4E4
Canada
www.lanaknits.com
888-302-0011

Karabella Yarns, Inc.
1201 Broadway
New York, NY 10001
www.karabellayarns.com
800-550-0898

KFI
P.O. Box 336
315 Bayview Ave.
Amityville, NY 11701
www.knittingfever.com
516-546-3600

Knit Picks
Crafts Americana Group, Inc.
13118 N.E. 4th St.
Vancouver, WA 98684
www.knitpicks.com
800-574-1323

Lion Brand Yarn
135 Kero Rd.
Carlstadt, NJ 07072
www.lionbrand.com
800-258-YARN

Lorna's Laces
4229 North Honore St.
Chicago, IL 60613
www.lornaslaces.net
773-935-3803

Louet Yarns
808 Commerce Park Dr.
Ogdensburg, NY 13669
www.louet.com
sales@louet.com

Mission Falls
5333 Casgrain #1204
Montreal, QC H2T 1X3
Canada
www.missionfalls.com
877-244-1204

Morehouse Merino
Morehouse Farm
141 Milan Hill Rd.
Red Hook, NY 12571
www.morehousefarm.com
866-470-4852

Nashua Yarns
Distributed by Westminster Fibers
www.westminsterfibers.com

Nature's Palette
Hand Jive Knits
www.handjiveknits.com
916-806-8063

Noro Yarn
Distributed by KFI
www.knittingfever.com

Peace Fleece
475 Porterfield Rd.
Porter, ME 04068
www.peacefleece.com
800-482-2841

Plymouth Yarn Co., Inc.
500 Lafayette St.
Bristol, PA 19007
www.plymouthyarn.com
215-788-0459

Rowan Yarn
Distributed by Westminster Fibers
www.knitrowan.com

Tahki • Stacy Charles, Inc.
70-30 80th St.
Building 36
Ridgewood, NY 11385
www.tahkistacycharles.com
800-338-YARN

Westminster Fibers
165 Ledge St.
Nashua, NH 03063
www.westminsterfibers.com
800-445-9276

REFERENCES

The following books were helpful in writing "Men in Knits: The First 800 Years"

Feitelson, Ann *The Art of Fair Isle Knitting* (Interweave Press, 1996)

Macdonald, Anne L. *No Idle Hands: A Social History of American Knitting* (Ballantine Books, 1988)

Rutt, Richard *A History of Hand Knitting* (Interweave Press, 1987)

van der Klift-Tellegen, Henriette *Knitting from the Netherlands: Traditional Dutch Fisherman's Sweaters* (Lark Books, 1985)

Index

Credits

PHOTO
page 8: (top) Victoria & Albert Museum, London/Art Resource; (bottom) Victoria & Albert Museum, London. **page 9:** photographer P. Dijkers. Collection Stadsarchief Vlaardingen, The Netherlands. **page 10:** 1925, Lander, John St. Helier (1869–1944)/Leeds Museums and Galleries (Lotherton Hall) U.K./The Bridgeman Art Library. **page 11:** (top) Library of Congress; (bottom) all Corbis.

FASHION
page 26: pants, T-shirt, and necklace, Urban Outfitters; motorcycle jacket, Trash & Vaudeville. **pages 31 & 33:** shirt and jacket, Triple 5 Soul. **pages 37 & 38:** (left) sneakers and hat, Ben Sherman; pants and T-shirt, Urban Outfitters; blazer, Diesel. (right) shoes, Fluevog; pants, Urban Outfitters; T-shirt, Subscript Samurai; blazer, Triple 5 Soul; sunglasses, Ben Sherman. **pages 39 & 40:** T-shirt, Urban Outfitters; jacket, Triple 5 Soul. **page 42:** shirt, Ben Sherman; peacoat, Urban Outfitters; pants, Triple 5 Soul. **page 47:** T-shirt, Urban Outfitters. **page 50:** T-shirt, Urban Outfitters; military shirt, A. Kurtz; jeans, Ben Sherman; belt, stylist's own. **pages 53 & 54:** shirt, stylist's own; jacket, Subscript. **pages 57 & 63:** jeans, T-shirt, and sneakers, Urban Outfitters; jacket, Carlos Campos; belt, stylist's own. **pages 64, 65 & 66:** shirt and belt, Urban Outfitters; coat and jeans, Ben Sherman. **page 68:** shirt and tie, Ben Sherman; blazer, Urban Outfitters; jeans, H&M. **page 73:** (left) shirt, Urban Outfitters; blazer, A. Kurtz; jeans, Ben Sherman. (right) jeans, H&M; hoodie, Paul Frank; jacket and jeans, Urban Outfitters. **pages 74, 77**

& 78: jeans, Ben Sherman. **page 81:** pants, Carlos Campos; T-shirt, Urban Outfitters; belt, stylist's own. **pages 84 & 86:** jeans, Ben Sherman. **page 89:** T-shirt, Urban Outfitters; jeans, Ben Sherman. **page 92:** jeans, Urban Outfitters; shirt, stylist's own. **page 97:** shirts, Urban Outfitters; pants, A. Kurtz. **page 102:** shirt, stylist's own; trousers, Carlos Campos. **pages 107 & 110:** shirt, Urban Outfitters; trousers, Standard Cloth. **pages 112, 115 & 116:** pants, Triple 5 Soul. **pages 119, 121 & 123:** pants, Triple 5 Soul. **pages 124 & 127:** T-shirt, Brooklyn Industries; jeans, Urban Outfitters. **pages 129 & 130:** jeans and sunglasses, Urban Outfitters; belt, stylist's own; messenger bag, A. Kurtz. **page 135:** shorts, Urban Outfitters; backpack, Triple 5 Soul. **pages 139 & 141:** pants, Urban Outfitters. **page 143:** shirt, tie, and jeans, Ben Sherman. **pages 147 & 149:** hat, Urban Outfitters; pants, H&M. **pages 150 & 157:** pants, Triple 5 Soul. **pages 159 & 162:** T-shirt, Brooklyn Industries; jeans, Urban Outfitters. **pages 171 & 173:** shirt, Urban Outfitters; pants, Ben Sherman; shoes, Fluevog. **pages 176 & 179:** jacket, Brooklyn Industries; hoodie, Triko; jeans, H&M; sneakers, Urban Outfitters; sunglasses, Ben Sherman. **page 181:** pants, Urban Outfitters; jacket, Trash & Vaudeville; shoes, Fluevog. **page 185:** shirt, Urban Outfitters; boxers, Ben Sherman. **page 191:** shirt, Carlos Campos; pants, Ben Sherman; shoes, Fluevog; hat, Trash & Vaudeville. **page 195:** (left) shirt, Polo Ralph Lauren; blazer, Urban Outfitters. (right) shirt and blazer, Ben Sherman. **pages 205 & 206:** (left) hoodie, Brooklyn Industries; peacoat, Ben Sherman; jeans, H&M; sneakers, Urban Outfitters. (right) T-shirt and coat, Brooklyn Industries; jeans and sneakers, Urban Outfitters.